RAPE

RAPE

The Politics
Of Consciousness

Susan Griffin

1817

Harper & Row, Publishers, San Francisco

Cambridge, Hagerstown, New York, Philadelphia, Washington
London, Mexico City, São Paulo, Singapore, Sydney

Library of Congress Cataloging-in-Publication Data

Griffin, Susan.
  Rape, the politics of consciousness.

  Rev. ed. of: Rape, the power of consciousness.
  1. Rape—United States. 2. Rape. I. Griffin,
Susan. Rape, the power of consciousness. II. Title.
HV6561.G74 1986   362.8'8   85–45738
ISBN 0–06–250351–0

86 87 88 89 90 MPC 10 9 8 7 6 5 4 3 2 1

CONTENTS

Acknowledgments   vii

ONE   Politics   1

TWO   A History   25

THREE   Consciousness   69

FOUR   The Power of Consciousness: A Collage   93
        with Sandy Boucher

Appendix: Rape Crisis Centers   139

ACKNOWLEDGMENTS

Lᴇᴛ ᴍᴇ ꜰɪʀsᴛ thank Michelle Cliff whose writing and thinking on the work of Simone Weil did much to shape the third essay
in this book. Sandy Boucher, who collaborated with me on the last
part of the book, was a sensitive reader who pointed out to me
much that needed to be said. The final section of the book would
never be as it is without the existence of so many women's pe-
riodicals, and so let me thank *Quest, Heresies, Chrysalis, Woman
Spirit, Ms, Sinister Wisdom, Conditions* and *Signs*. This work
would also not have been possible had we not been able to use the
Women's History Library as collected by Laura X, part of which
is kept on microfilm at the Berkeley Public Library. Let me also
thank June Jordan and Adrienne Rich for reading and commenting
on the third essay in this book and for their support, and Kim
Chernin who read this book and helped to make a significant decision with regard to its form. I wish also to thank Gilda Grillo,
Lois Sasson, Rezaleah Bat Pinchas and Bob Hoffmann and the
Quadrinity Process for their friendship, support and for certain
transforming insights which have found their way into this writing.
Let me also thank Professor Menachem Amir who consulted with
me in 1970 when I wrote the first essay on rape that appears in
this book. And finally I would like to thank Marie Cantlon for her
intelligent and invaluable editing and for her patience.

For this third edition of the book I would like to thank John
Loudon for his insights and support; Janet Reed for her assistance;
and Pat Ellsberg and Claire Greensfelder for reading the manuscript
and offering helpful responses. I would also like to thank Teresa
Bacon for her assistance with research.

In order that we stop being victims, we ourselves must take up the struggle against rape. Individually and collectively we can break the silence and make it no longer a taboo subject, or something shameful which weighs us down.

French witness. *The Proceedings of the International Tribunal on Crimes Against Women.* Diana E. H. Russell and Nicole Van de Ven (Eds.).

Martial arts and self defense study offer a way of self reflection and change . . . I find that I learned the lessons of patriarchy in my muscles and sinews, as well as in my mind and soul; and this martial arts study is both an UNconditioning process, as well as the conditioning and creating of a new self.

Emily Erwin Culpepper, *Womanspirit,* Summer, 1976

She looked up over her knitting and met the third stroke and it seemed to her like her own eyes meeting her own eyes, searching as she could alone search into her mind and her heart, purifying out of existence that lie, any lie. She praised herself in praising the light, without vanity, for she was stern, she was searching, she was beautiful like that light.

Virginia Woolf. *To the Lighthouse*

PART ONE

Politics
1971

I

I have never been free of the fear of rape. From a very early age I, like most women, have thought of rape as part of my natural environment—something to be feared and prayed against like fire or lightning. I never asked why men raped; I simply thought it one of the many mysteries of human nature.

I was, however, curious enough about the violent side of humanity to read every crime magazine I was able to ferret away from my grandfather. Each issue featured at least one "sex crime," with pictures of a victim, usually in a pearl necklace, and of the ditch or the orchard where her body was found. I was never certain why the victims were always women, nor what the motives of the murderer were, but I did guess that the world was not a safe place for women. I observed that my grandmother was meticulous about locks, and quick to draw the shades before anyone removed so much as a shoe. I sensed that danger lurked outside.

At the age of eight, my suspicions were confirmed. My grandmother took me to the back of the house where the men wouldn't hear, and told me that strange men wanted to do harm to little girls. I learned not to walk on dark streets, not to talk to strangers, or get into strange cars, to lock doors, and to be modest. She never explained why a man would want to harm a little girl, and I never asked.

If I thought for a while that my grandmother's fears were imaginary, the illusion was brief. That year, on the way home from school, a schoolmate a few years older than I tried to rape me. Later, in an obscure aisle of the local library (while I was reading *Freddy the Pig*) I turned to discover a man exposing himself. Then, the friendly man around the corner was arrested for child molesting.

My initiation to sexuality was typical. Every woman has similar stories to tell—the first man who attacked her may have been a neighbor, a family friend, an uncle, her doctor, or perhaps her own father. And women who grow up in New York City always have tales about the subway.

But though rape and the fear of rape are a daily part of every woman's consciousness, the subject is so rarely discussed by that unofficial staff of male intellectuals (who write the books which study seemingly every other form of male activity) that one begins to suspect a conspiracy of silence. And indeed, the obscurity of rape in print exists in marked contrast to the frequency of rape in reality, for *forcible rape is the most frequently committed violent crime in America today.* The Federal Bureau of Investigation classes three crimes as violent: murder, aggravated assault and forcible rape. In 1968, 31,060 rapes were *reported.* According to the FBI and independent criminologists, however, to approach accuracy this figure must be multiplied by at least a factor of ten to compensate for the fact that most rapes are not reported; when these compensatory mathematics are used, there are more rapes committed than aggravated assaults and homicides.

When I asked Berkeley California's Police Inspector in charge of rape investigation if he knew why men rape women, he replied that he had not spoken with "these people and delved into what really makes them tick, because that really isn't my job. . . ." However, when I asked him how a woman might prevent being raped, he was not so reticent, "I wouldn't advise any female to go walking around alone at night . . . and she should lock her car at all times." The Inspector illustrated his warning with a grisly story about a man who lay in wait for women in the back seats of their cars, while they were shopping in a local supermarket. This man eventually murdered one of his rape victims. "Always lock your car," the Inspector repeated, and then added, without a hint of irony, "Of course, you don't have to be paranoid about this type of thing."

The Inspector wondered why I wanted to write about rape. Like most men he did not understand the urgency of the topic, for, after all, men are not raped. But like most women I had spent considerable time speculating on the true nature of the rapist. When I was very young, my image of the "sexual offender" was a nightmarish amalgamation of the bogey man and Captain Hook: he wore a black cape, and he cackled. As I matured, so did my image of the rapist. Born into the psychoanalytic age, I tried to "understand" the rapist. Rape, I came to believe, was only one of many unfortunate evils produced by sexual repression. Reasoning by tautology, I concluded that any man who would rape a woman must be out of his mind.

Yet, though the theory that rapists are insane is a popular one, this belief has no basis in fact. According to Professor Menachem Amir's study of 646 rape cases in Philadelphia, *Patterns in Forcible Rape*, men who rape are not abnormal. Amir writes, "Studies indicate that sex offenders do not constitute a unique or psychopathological type; nor are they as a group invariably more disturbed than the control groups to which they are compared." Alan Taylor, a parole officer who has worked with rapists in the prison facilities at San Luis Obispo, California, stated the question in plainer language, "Those men were the most normal men there. They had a lot of hang-ups, but they were the same hang-ups as men walking out on the street."

Another canon in the apologetics of rape is that, if it were not for learned social controls, all men would rape. Rape is held to be natural behavior, and not to rape must be learned. But in truth rape is not universal to the human species. Moreover, studies of rape in our culture reveal that, far from being impulsive behavior, most rape is planned. Professor Amir's study reveals that in cases of group rape—(the "gangbang" of masculine slang) 90 percent of the rapes were planned; in pair rapes, 83 percent of the rapes were planned; and in single rapes, 58 percent were planned. These figures should significantly discredit the image of the rapist as a man who is suddenly overcome by sexual needs society does not allow him to fulfill.

Far from the social control of rape being learned, comparisons with other cultures lead one to suspect that, in our society, it is rape itself that is learned. (The fact that rape is against the law should not be considered proof that rape is not in fact encouraged as part of our culture.)

This culture's concept of rape as an illegal, but still understandable, form of behavior is not a universal one. In her study *Sex and Temperament,* Margaret Mead describes a society that does not share our views. The Arapesh do not ". . . have any conception of the male nature that might make rape understandable to them." Indeed our interpretation of rape is a product of our conception of the nature of male sexuality. A common retort to the question, why don't women rape men, is the myth that men have greater sexual needs, that their sexuality is more urgent than women's. And it is the nature of human beings to want to live up to what is expected of them.

And this same culture which expects aggression from the male expects passivity from the female. Conveniently, the companion myth about the nature of female sexuality is that all women secretly want to be raped. Lurking beneath her modest female exterior is a subconscious desire to be ravished. The following description of a stag movie, written by Brenda Starr in Los Angeles' underground paper, *Everywoman,* typifies this male fantasy. The movie "showed a woman in her underclothes reading on her bed. She is interrupted by a rapist with a knife. He immediately wins her over with his charm and they get busy sucking and fucking." An advertisement in the *Berkeley Barb* reads, "Now as all women know from their daydreams, rape has a lot of advantages. Best of all it's so simple. No preparation necessary, no planning ahead of time, no wondering if you should or shouldn't; just whang! bang!" Thanks to Masters and Johnson even the scientific canon recognizes that for the female, "whang! bang!" can scarcely be described as pleasurable.

Still, the male psyche persists in believing that, protestations and struggles to the contrary, deep inside her mysterious feminine soul, the female victim has wished for her own fate. A young woman who was raped by the husband of a friend said that days after the incident the man returned to her home, pounded on the door and screamed to her, "Jane, Jane. You loved it. You know you loved it."

The theory that women like being raped extends itself by deduction into the proposition that most or much of rape is provoked by the victim. But this too is only myth. Though provocation, considered a mitigating factor in a court of law, may consist of only "a gesture," according to the Federal Commission on Crimes of Violence, only 4 percent of reported rapes involved any precipitative behavior by the woman.

The notion that rape is enjoyed by the victim is also convenient for the man who, though he would not commit forcible rape, enjoys the idea of its existence, as if rape confirms that enormous sexual potency which he secretly knows to be his own. It is for the pleasure of the armchair rapist that detailed accounts of violent rapes exist in the media. Indeed, many men appear to take sexual pleasure from nearly all forms of violence. Whatever the motivation, male sexuality and violence in our culture seem to be inseparable. James Bond alternately whips out his revolver and his cock, and though there is no known connection between the skills of gunfighting and lovemaking, pacifism seems suspiciously effeminate.

In a recent fictional treatment of the Manson case, Frank Conroy writes of his vicarious titillation when describing the murders to his wife:

"Every single person there was killed." She didn't move.

"It sounds like there was torture," I said. As the words left my mouth I knew there was no need to say them to frighten her into believing that she needed me for protection.

The pleasure he feels as his wife's protector is inextricably mixed with pleasure in the violence itself. Conroy writes, "I was excited by the killings, as one excited by catastrophe on a grand scale, as one is alert to pre-echoes of unknown changes, hints of unrevealed secrets, rumblings of chaos. . . ."

The attraction of the male in our culture to violence and death is a tradition Manson and his admirers are carrying on with tireless avidity (even presuming Manson's innocence, he dreams of the purification of fire and destruction). It was Malraux in his *Anti-Memoirs* who said that, for the male, facing death was the illuminating experience analogous to childbirth for the female. Certainly our culture does glorify war and shroud the agonies of the gunfighter in veils of mystery.

And in the spectrum of male behavior, rape, the perfect combination of sex and violence, is the penultimate act. Erotic pleasure cannot be separated from culture, and in our culture male eroticism is wedded to power. Not only should a man be taller and stronger than a female in the perfect love-match, but he must also demonstrate his superior strength in gestures of dominance which are perceived as amorous. Though the law attempts to make a clear division between rape and sexual intercourse, in fact the courts find it difficult to distinguish between a case where the decision to copulate was mutual and one where a man forced himself upon his partner.

The scenario is even further complicated by the expectation that, not only does a woman mean "yes" when she says "no," but that a really decent woman ought to begin by saying "no," and then be led down the primrose path to acquiescence. Ovid, the author of Western Civilization's most celebrated sex manual, makes this expectation perfectly clear:

. . . and when I beg you to say "yes," say "no." Then let me lie outside your bolted door. . . . So Love grows strong. . . .

That the basic elements of rape are involved in all heterosexual relationships may explain why men often identify with the offender in this crime. But to regard the rapist as the victim, a man driven by his inherent sexual needs to take what will not be given him, reveals a basic ignorance of sexual politics. For in our culture heterosexual love finds an erotic expression through male dominance and female submission. A man who derives pleasure from raping a woman clearly must enjoy force and dominance as much or more than the simple pleasures of the flesh. Coitus cannot be experienced in isolation. The weather, the state of the nation, the level of sugar in the blood—all will affect a man's ability to achieve orgasm. If a man can achieve sexual pleasure after terrorizing and humiliating the object of his passion, and in fact while inflicting pain upon her, one must assume he derives pleasure directly from terrorizing, humiliating and harming a woman. According to Amir's study of forcible rape, on a statistical average the man who has been convicted of rape was found to have a normal sexual personality, tending to be different from the normal, well-adjusted male only in having a greater tendency to express violence and rage.

And if the professional rapist is to be separated from the average dominant heterosexual, it may be mainly a quantitative difference. For the existence of rape as an index to masculinity is not entirely metaphorical. Though this measure of masculinity seems to be more publicly exhibited among "bad boys" or aging bikers who practice sexual initiation through group rape, in fact, "good boys" engage in the same rites to prove their manhood. In Stockton, a small town in California which epitomizes silent-majority America, a bachelor party was given last summer for a young man about to be married. A woman was hired to dance "topless" for the amusement of the guests. At the high point of the evening the bridegroom-to-be dragged the woman into a bedroom. No move was made by any of his companions to stop what was clearly going to be an attempted rape. Far from it. As the woman described, "I tried to keep him away—told him of my Herpes Genitalis, et cetera, but he couldn't face the guys if he didn't screw me." After the bridegroom had finished raping the woman and returned with her to the party, far from chastising him, his friends heckled the woman and covered her with wine.

It was fortunate for the dancer that the bridegroom's friends did not follow him into the bedroom for, though one might suppose that in group rape, since the victim is outnumbered, less force would be inflicted on her, in fact, Amir's studies indicate, "the most excessive degrees of violence occurred in group rape." Far from discouraging violence, the presence of other men may in fact encourage sadism, and even cause the behavior. In an unpublished study of group rape by Gilbert Geis and Duncan Chappell, the authors refer to a study by W. H. Blanchard which relates,

The leader of the male group . . . apparently precipitated and maintained the activity, despite misgivings, because of a need to fulfill the role that the other two men had assigned to him. "I was scared when it began to happen," he says. "I wanted to leave but I didn't want to say it to the other guys—you know—that I was scared."

Thus it becomes clear that not only does our culture teach men the rudiments of rape, but society, or more specifically other men, encourage the practice of it.

II

Every man I meet wants to protect me. Can't figure out what from.
—Mac West

If a male society rewards aggressive, domineering sexual behavior, it contains within itself a sexual schizophrenia. For the masculine man is also expected to prove his mettle as a protector of women. To the naive eye, this dichotomy implies that men fall into one of two categories: those who rape and those who protect. In fact, life does not prove so simple. In a study euphemistically entitled "Sex Aggression by College Men," it was discovered that men who believe in a double standard of morality for men and women, who in fact believe most fervently in the ultimate value of virginity, are more liable to commit "this aggressive variety of sexual exploitation."

(At this point in our narrative it should come as no surprise that Sir Thomas Malory, creator of that classic tale of chivalry, *The Knights of the Round Table,* was himself arrested and found guilty for repeated incidents of rape.)

In the system of chivalry, men protect women against men. This is not unlike the protection relationship which the mafia established with small businesses in the early part of this century. Indeed, chivalry is an age-old protection racket which depends for its existence on rape.

According to the male mythology which defines and perpetuates rape, it is an animal instinct inherent in the male. The story goes that sometime in our pre-historical past, the male, more hirsute and burly than today's counterparts, roamed about an uncivilized landscape until he found a desirable female. (Oddly enough, this female is *not* pictured as more muscular than the modern woman.) Her mate does not bother with courtship. He simply grabs her by the hair and drags her to the closest cave. Presumably, one of the major advantages of modern civilization for the female has been the civilizing of the male. We call it chivalry.

But women do not get chivalry for free. According to the logic of sexual politics, we too have to civilize our behavior. (Enter chastity. Enter virginity. Enter monogamy.) For the female, civilized behavior means chastity before marriage and faithfulness within it. Chivalrous behavior in the male is supposed to protect that chastity from involuntary defilement. The fly in the ointment of this otherwise peaceful system is the fallen woman. She does not behave. And therefore she does not deserve protection. Or, to use another argument, a major tenet of the same value system: what has once been defiled cannot again be violated. One begins to suspect that it is the behavior of the fallen woman, and not that of the male, that civilization aims to control.

The assumption that a woman who does not respect the double standard deserves whatever she gets (or at the very least "asks for it") operates in the courts today. While in some states a man's previous rape convictions are not considered admissible evidence, the sexual reputation of the rape victim is considered a crucial element of the facts upon which the court must decide innocence or guilt.

The court's respect for the double standard manifested itself particularly clearly in the case of the People v. Jerry Plotkin. Mr. Plotkin, a 36-year-old jeweler, was tried for rape last spring in a San Francisco Superior Court. According to the woman who brought the charges, Plotkin, along with three other men, forced her at gunpoint to enter a car one night in October 1970. She was taken to Mr. Plotkin's fashionable apartment where he and the three other men first raped her and then, in the delicate language of the *S.F. Chronicle*, "subjected her to perverted sex acts." She was, she said, set free in the morning with the warning that she would be killed if she spoke to anyone about the event. She did report the incident to the police who then searched Plotkin's apartment and discovered a long list of names of women. Her name was on the list and had been crossed out.

In addition to the woman's account of her abduction and rape, the prosecution submitted four of Plotkin's address books containing the names of hundreds of women. Plotkin claimed he did not know all of the women since some of the names had been given to him by friends and he had not yet called on them. Several women, however, did testify in court that Plotkin had, to cite the *Chronicle*, "lured them up to his apartment under one pretext or another, and forced his sexual attentions on them."

Plotkin's defense rested on two premises. First, through his own testimony Plotkin established a reputation for himself as a sexual libertine who frequently picked up girls in bars and took them to his house where sexual relations often took place. He was the Playboy. He claimed that the accusation of rape, therefore, was false—this incident had simply been one of many casual sexual relationships, the victim one of many playmates. The second premise of the defense was that his accuser was also a sexual libertine. However, the picture created of the young woman (fully 13 years younger than Plotkin) was not akin to the light-hearted, gay-bachelor image projected by the defendant. On the contrary, the day after the defense cross-examined the woman, the *Chronicle* printed a story headlined, "Grueling Day for Rape Case Victim." (A leaflet passed out by women in front of the courtroom was more succinct, "rape was committed by four men in a private apartment in October; on Thursday, it was done by a judge and a lawyer in a public courtroom.")

Through skillful questioning fraught with innuendo, Plotkin's defense attorney James Martin MacInnis portrayed the young woman as a licentious opportunist and unfit mother. MacInnis began by asking the young woman (then employed as a secretary) whether or not it was true that she was "familiar with liquor" and had worked as a "cocktail waitress." The young woman replied (the *Chronicle* wrote "admitted") that she had worked once or twice as a cocktail waitress. The attorney then asked if she had worked as a secretary in the financial district but had "left that employment after it was discovered that you had sexual intercourse on a couch in the office." The woman replied, "That is a lie. I left because I didn't like working in a one-girl office. It was too lonely." Then the defense asked if, while working as an attendant at a health club, "you were accused of having a sexual affair with a man?" Again the woman denied the story, "I was never accused of that."

Plotkin's attorney then sought to establish that his client's accuser was living with a married man. She responded that the man was separated from his wife. Finally he told the court that she had "spent the night" with another man who lived in the same building.

At this point in the testimony the woman asked Plotkin's defense attorney, "Am I on trial? . . . It is embarrassing and personal to admit these things to all these people. . . . I did not commit a crime. I am a human being." The lawyer, true to the chivalry of his class, apologized and immediately resumed questioning her, turning his attention to her children. (She is divorced, and the children at the time of the trial were in a foster home.) "Isn't it true that your two children have a sex game in which one gets on top of another and they—"That is a lie!" the young woman interrupted him. She ended her testimony by explaining, "They are wonderful children. They are not perverted."

The jury, divided in favor of acquittal ten to two, asked the court stenographer to read the woman's testimony back to them. After this reading, the Superior Court acquitted the defendant of both charges of rape and kidnapping.

According to the double standard a woman who has had sexual intercourse out of wedlock cannot be raped. Rape is not only a crime of aggression against the body; it is a transgression against chastity as defined by men. When a woman is forced into a sexual relationship, she has, according to the male ethos, been violated. But she is also defiled if she does not behave according to the double standard, by maintaining her chastity, or confining her sexual activities to a monogamous relationship.

One should not assume, however, that a woman can avoid the possibility of rape simply by behaving. Though myth would have it that mainly "bad girls" are raped, this theory has no basis in fact. Available statistics would lead one to believe that a safer course is promiscuity. In a study of rape done in the District of Columbia, it was found that 82 percent of the rape victims had a "good reputation." Even the Police Inspector's advice to stay off the streets is rather useless, for almost half of reported rapes occur in the home of the victim and are committed by a man she has never before seen. Like indiscriminate terrorism, rape can happen to any woman, and few women are ever without this knowledge.

But the courts and the police, both dominated by white males, continue to suspect the rape victim, *sui generis*, of provoking or asking for her own assault. According to Amir's study, the police tend to believe that a woman without a good reputation cannot be raped. The rape victim is usually submitted to countless questions about her own sexual mores and behavior by the police. This preoccupation is partially justified by the legal requirements for prosecution in a rape case. The rape victim must have been penetrated, and she must have made it clear to her assailant that she did not want penetration (unless of course she is unconscious). A refusal to accompany a man to some isolated place to allow him to touch her does not in the eyes of the court, constitute rape. She must have said "no" at the crucial genital moment. And the rape victim, to qualify as such, must also have put up a physical struggle—unless she can prove that to do so would have been to endanger her life.

But the zealous interest the police frequently exhibit in the physical details of a rape case is only partially explained by the requirements of the court. A woman who was raped in Berkeley was asked to tell the story of her rape four different times "right out in the street," while her assailant was escaping. She was then required to submit to a pelvic examination to prove that penetration had taken place. Later, she was taken to the police station where she was asked the same questions again: "Were you forced?" "Did he penetrate?" "Are you sure your life was in danger and you had no other choice?" This woman had been pulled off the street by a man who held a 10-inch knife at her throat and forcibly raped her. She was raped at midnight and was not able to return to her home until five in the morning. Police contacted her twice again in the next week, once by telephone at two in the morning and once at four in the morning. In her words, "The rape was probably the least traumatic incident of the whole evening. If I'm ever raped again, . . . I wouldn't report it to the police because of all the degradation. . . ."

If white women are subjected to unnecessary and often hostile questioning after having been raped, third world women are often not believed at all. According to the white male ethos (which is not only sexist but racist), third world women are defined from birth as "impure." Thus the white male is provided with a pool of women who are fair game for sexual imperialism. Third world women frequently do not report rape and for good reason. When blues singer Billie Holliday was 10 years old, she was taken off to a local house by a neighbor and raped. Her mother brought the police to rescue her, and she was taken to the local police station crying and bleeding:

When we got there, instead of treating me and Mom like somebody who called the cops for help, they treated me like I'd killed somebody. . . . I guess they had me figured for having enticed this old goat into the whorehouse. . . . All I know for sure is they threw me into a cell . . . a fat white matron . . . saw I was still bleeding, she felt sorry for me and gave me a couple glasses of milk. But nobody else did anything for me except give me filthy looks and snicker to themselves.

After a couple of days in a cell they dragged me into a court. Mr. Dick got sentenced to five years. They sentenced me to a Catholic institution.

Clearly the white man's chivalry is aimed only to protect the chastity of "his" women.

As a final irony, that same system of sexual values from which chivalry is derived has also provided womankind with an unwritten code of behavior, called femininity, which makes a feminine woman the perfect victim of sexual aggression. If being chaste does not ward off the possibility of assault, being feminine certainly increases the chances that it will succeed. To be submissive is to defer to masculine strength; is to lack muscular development or any interest in defending oneself; is to let doors be opened, to have one's arm held when crossing the street. To be feminine is to wear shoes which make it difficult to run; skirts which inhibit one's stride; underclothes which inhibit the circulation. Is it not an intriguing observation that those very clothes which are thought to be flattering to the female and attractive to the male are those which make it impossible for a woman to defend herself against aggression?

Each girl as she grows into womanhood is taught fear. Fear is the form in which the female internalizes both chivalry and the double standard. Since, biologically speaking, women in fact have the same if not greater potential for sexual expression as do men, the woman who is taught that she must behave differently from a man must also learn to distrust her own carnality. She must deny her own feelings and learn not to act from them. She fears herself. This is the essence of passivity and, of course, a woman's passivity is not simply sexual but functions to cripple her from self-expression in every area of her life.

Passivity itself prevents a woman from ever considering her own potential for self-defense and forces her to look to men for protection. The woman is taught fear, but this time fear of the other; and yet her only relief from this fear is to seek out the other. Moreover, the passive woman is taught to regard herself as impotent, unable to act, unable even to perceive, in no way self-sufficient, and finally, as the object and not the subject of human behavior. It is in this sense that a woman is deprived of the status of a human being. She is not free to be.

III

Since Ibsen's Nora slammed the door on her patriarchical husband, woman's attempt to be free has been more or less fashionable. In this nineteenth-century portrait of a woman leaving her marriage, Nora tells her husband, "Our home has been nothing but a playroom. I have been your doll-wife just as at home I was papa's doll-child." And, at least on the stage, "The Doll's House" crumbled, leaving audiences with hope for the fate of the modern woman. And today, as in the past, womankind has not lacked examples of liberated women to emulate: Emma Goldman, Greta Garbo and Isadora Duncan all denounced marriage and the double standard, and believed their right to freedom included sexual independence; but still their example has not affected the lives of millions of women who continue to marry, divorce and remarry, living out their lives dependent on the status and economic power of men. Patriarchy still holds the average woman prisoner not because she lacks the courage of an Isadora Duncan, but because the material conditions of her life prevent her from being anything but an object.

In the *Elementary Structures of Kinship*, Claude Levi-Strauss gives to marriage this universal description, "It is always a system of exchange that we find at the origin of the rules of marriage." In this system of exchange, a woman is the "most precious possession." Levi-Strauss continues that the custom of including women as booty in the marketplace is still so general that "a whole volume would not be sufficient to enumerate instances of it." Levi-Strauss makes it clear that he does not exclude Western Civilization from his definition of "universal" and cites examples from modern wedding ceremonies. (The marriage ceremony is still one in which the husband and wife become one, and "that one is the husband.")

The legal proscription against rape reflects this possessory view of women. An article in the 1952–53 *Yale Law Journal* describes the legal rationale behind laws against rape:

> In our society sexual taboos, often enacted into law, buttress a system of monogamy based upon the law of "free-bargaining" of the potential spouses. Within this process the woman's power to withhold or grant sexual access is an important bargaining weapon.

Presumably then, laws against rape are intended to protect the right of a woman, not for physical self-determination, but for physical "bargaining." The article goes on to explain explicitly why the preservation of the bodies of women is important to men:

> The consent standard in our society does more than protect a significant item of social currency for women; it fosters, and is in turn bolstered by, a masculine pride in the exclusive possession of a sexual object. The consent of a woman to sexual intercourse awards the man a privilege of bodily access, a personal "prize," whose value is enhanced by sole ownership. An additional reason for the man's condemnation of rape may be found in the threat to his status from a decrease in the "value" of his sexual possession which would result from forcible violation.

The passage concludes by making clear whose interest the law is designed to protect. "The man responds to this undercutting of his status as *possessor* of the girl with hostility toward the rapist; no other restitution device is available. The law of rape provides an orderly outlet for his vengeance." Presumably the female victim in any case will have been sufficiently socialized so as not to consciously feel any strong need for vengeance. If she does feel this need, society does not speak of it.

The laws against rape exist to protect rights of the male as possessor of the female body, and not the right of the female over her own body. Even without this enlightening passage from the *Yale Law Review*, the laws themselves are clear: In no state can a man be accused of raping his wife. How can any man steal what already belongs to him? It is in the sense of rape as theft of another man's property that Kate Millett writes, "Traditionally rape has been viewed as an offense one male commits against another—a matter of abusing his woman." In raping another man's woman, a man may aggrandize his own manhood and concurrently reduce that of another man. Thus a man's honor is not subject directly to rape, but only indirectly, through "his" woman.

If the basic social unit is the family, in which the woman is a possession of her husband, the superstructure of society is a male hierarchy, in which men dominate other men (or patriarchal families dominate other patriarchal families). And it is no small irony that, while the very social fabric of our male-dominated culture denies women equal access to political, economic and legal power, the literature, myth and humor of our culture depict women not only as the power behind the throne, but the real source of the oppression of men. The religious version of this fairy tale blames Eve for both carnality and eating of the tree of knowledge, at the same time making her gullible to the obvious devices of a serpent. Adam, of course, is merely the trusting victim of love. Certainly this is a biased story. But no more biased than the one television audiences receive today from the latest slick comedians. Through a media which is owned by men, censored by a state dominated by men, all the evils of this social system which make a man's life unpleasant are blamed upon "the wife." The theory is: were it not for the female who waits and plots to "trap" the male into marriage, modern man would be able to achieve Olympian freedom. She is made the scapegoat for a system which is in fact run by men.

Nowhere is this more clear than in the white racist use of the concept of white womanhood. The white male's open rape of black women, coupled with his overweening concern for the chastity and protection of his wife and daughters, represents an extreme of sexist and racist hypocrisy. While on the one hand she was held up as the standard for purity and virtue, on the other the Southern white woman was never asked if she wanted to be on a pedestal, and in fact any deviance from the male-defined standards for white womanhood was treated severely. (It is a powerful commentary on American racism that the historical role of Blacks as slaves, and thus possessions without power, has robbed black women of legal and economic protection through marriage. Thus black women in Southern society and in the ghettoes of the North have long been easy game for white rapists.) The fear that black men would rape white women was classic paranoia. Quoting from Ann Breen's unpublished study of racism and sexism in the South, "The New South: White Man's Country," Frederick Douglass legitimately points out that, had the black man wished to rape white women, he had ample opportunity to do so during the Civil War when white women, the wives, sisters, daughters and mothers of the rebels, were left in the care of Blacks. But yet not a single act of rape was committed during this time. The Ku Klux Klan, who tarred and feathered black men and lynched them in the honor of the purity of white womanhood, also applied tar and feathers to a Southern white woman accused of bigamy, which leads one to suspect that Southern white men were not so much outraged at the violation of the woman as a person, in the few instances where rape was actually committed by black men, but at the violation of his property rights. In the situation where a black man was found to be having sexual relations with a white woman, the white woman could exercise skin-privilege, and claim that she had been raped in which case the black man was lynched. But if she did not claim rape, she herself was subject to lynching.

In constructing the myth of white womanhood so as to justify the lynching and oppression of black men and women, the white male has created a convenient symbol of his own power which has resulted in black hostility toward the white "bitch," accompanied by a fear on the part of many white women of the black rapist. Moreover, it is not surprising that after being told for two centuries that he wants to rape white women, black men have begun to actually commit that act. But it is crucial to note that the frequency of this practice is outrageously exaggerated in the white mythos. Ninety percent of reported rape is intra- not inter-racial.

In *Soul on Ice*, Eldridge Cleaver has described the mixing of a rage against white power with the internalized sexism of a black man raping a white woman.

Somehow I arrived at the conclusion that, as a matter of principle, it was of paramount importance for me to have an antagonistic, ruthless attitude toward white women. . . . Rape was an insurrectionary act. It delighted me that I was defying and trampling upon the white man's law, upon his system of values and that I was defiling his women—and this point, I believe, was the most satisfying to me because I was very resentful over the historical fact of how the white man has used the black woman.

Thus a black man uses white women to take out his rage against white men. But, in fact, whenever a rape of a white woman by a black man does take place, it is again the white man who benefits. First, the act itself terrorizes the white woman and makes her more dependent on the white male for protection. Then, if the woman prosecutes her attacker, the white man is afforded legal opportunity to exercise overt racism. Of course, the knowledge of the rape helps to perpetuate two myths which are beneficial to white male rule— the bestiality of the black man and the desirability of white women. Finally, the white man surely benefits because he himself is not the object of attack—he has been allowed to stay in power.

Indeed, the existence of rape in any form is beneficial to the ruling class of white males. For rape is a kind of terrorism which severely limits the freedom of women and makes women dependent on men. Moreover, in the act of rape, the rage that one man may harbor toward another higher in the male hierarchy can be deflected toward a female scapegoat. For every man there is always someone lower on the social scale on whom he can take out his aggressions. And that is any woman alive.

This oppressive attitude towards women finds its institutionalization in the traditional family. For it is assumed that a man "wears the pants" in his family—he exercises the option of rule whenever he so chooses. Not that he makes all the decisions—clearly women make most of the important day-to-day decisions in a family. But when a conflict of interest arises, it is the man's interest which will prevail. His word, in itself, is more powerful. He lords it over his wife in the same way his boss lords it over him, so that the very process of exercising his power becomes as important an act as obtaining whatever it is his power can get for him. This notion of power is key to the male ego in this culture, for the two acceptable measures of masculinity are a man's power over women and his power over other men. A man may boast to his friends that "I have 20 men working for me." It is also aggrandizement of his ego if he has the financial power to clothe his wife in furs and jewels. And, if a man lacks the wherewithal to acquire such power, he can always express his rage through equally masculine activities—rape and theft. Since male society defines the female as a possession, it is not surprising that the felony most often committed together with rape is theft. As the following classic tale of rape points out, the elements of theft, violence and forced sexual relations merge into an indistinguishable whole.

The woman who told the following story was acquainted with the man who tried to rape her. When the man learned that she was going to be staying alone for the weekend, he began early in the day a polite campaign to get her to go out with him. When she continued to refuse his request, his chivalrous mask dropped away:

I had locked all the doors because I was afraid, and I don't know how he got in; it was probably through the screen door. When I woke up, he was shaking my leg. His eyes were red, and I knew he had been drinking and smoking. I thought I would try to talk my way out of it. He started by saying that he wanted to sleep with me, and then he got angrier and angrier, until he started to say, "I want pussy," "I want pussy." Then, I got scared and tried to push him away. That's when he started to force himself on me. It was awful. It was the most humiliating, terrible feeling. He was forcing my legs apart and ripping my clothes off. And it was painful. I did fight him—he was slightly drunk and I was able to keep him away. I had taken judo a few years back, but I was afraid to throw a chop for fear that he'd kill me. I could see he was getting more and more violent. I was thinking wildly of some way to get out of this alive, and then I said to him, "Do you want money? I'll give you money." We had money but I was also thinking that if I got to the back room I could telephone the police—as if the police would have even helped. It was a stupid thing to think of because obviously he would follow me. And he did. When he saw me pick up the phone, he tried to tie the cord around my neck. I screamed at him that I did have the money in another room, that I was going to call the police because I was scared, but that I would never tell anybody what happened. It would be an absolute secret. He said, "okay," and I went to get the money. But when he got it, all of a sudden he got this crazy look in his eye and he said to me, "Now I'm going to kill you." Then I started saying my prayers. I knew there was nothing I could do. He started to hit me—I still wasn't sure if he wanted to rape me at this point—or just to kill me. He was hurting me, but hadn't yet gotten me into a stranglehold because he was still drunk and off balance. Somehow we pushed into the kitchen where I kept looking at this big knife. But I didn't pick it up. Somehow, no matter how much I hated him at that moment, I still couldn't imagine putting the knife in his flesh, and then I was afraid he would grab it and stick it into me. Then he was hitting me again and somehow we pushed through the back door of the kitchen and onto the porch steps. We fell down the steps and that's when he started to strangle me. He was on top of me. He just went on and on until finally I lost consciousness. I did scream, though my screams sounded like whispers to me. But what happened was that a cab driver happened by and frightened him away. The cab driver revived me—I was out only a minute at the most. And then I ran across the street and I grabbed the woman who was our neighbor and screamed at her, "Am I alive? Am I still alive?"

Rape is an act of aggression in which the victim is denied her self-determination. It is an act of violence which, if not actually followed by beatings or murder, nevertheless always carries with it the threat of death. And finally, rape is a form of mass terrorism, for the victims of rape are chosen indiscriminately, but the propagandists for male supremacy broadcast that it is women who cause rape by being unchaste or in the wrong place at the wrong time—in essence, by behaving as though they were free.

The threat of rape is used to deny women employment. (In California, the Berkeley Public Library, until pushed by the Federal Employment Practices Commission, refused to hire female shelvers because of perverted men in the stacks.) The fear of rape keeps women off the streets at night. Keeps women at home. Keeps women passive and modest for fear that they be thought provocative.

It is part of human dignity to be able to defend oneself, and women are learning. Some women have learned karate; some to shoot guns. And yet we will not be free until the threat of rape and the atmosphere of violence is ended, and to end that the nature of male behavior must change.

But rape is not an isolated act that can be rooted out from patriarchy without ending patriarchy itself. The same men and power structure who victimize women are engaged in the act of raping Vietnam, raping Black people and the very earth we live upon. Rape is a classic act of domination where, in the words of Kate Millett, "the emotions of hatred, contempt, and the desire to break or violate personality," take place. This breaking of the personality characterizes modern life itself. No simple reforms can eliminate rape. As the symbolic expression of the white male hierarchy, rape is the quintessential act of our civilization, one which, Valerie Solanis warns, is in danger of "humping itself to death."

PART TWO

A History
1971–1978

I

1971. For me a year of rages. We rose like a chorus of Erinyes. The furies. All that had been held back, the stories we never told; what we did not see or refused to recognize. And none of us alone in this. Now any woman, a neighbor, one's blood relatives, strangers had become allies, part of an unspoken network of thought. A whole new connective tissue began to grow between each of us and the women around us and a past we now claimed as our own and the lives of our daughters, or girls unborn which we wanted to imagine as different from our own, unscarred, not damaged by the list of atrocities we could suddenly now name.

And what is to be remembered is that before this eight years we have lived through since, much of what was the actuality of our lives went unnamed. We did not speak of rape. If a woman was raped she was supposed to feel ashamed. She *was* shamed. The very atmosphere around her said that she had been violated and damaged like property, that she must have wanted this rape, drawn this to her. And the atmosphere, like rape itself, seemed as if it had existed forever, were a natural phenomenon, and not made up of man-made assumptions and prejudices born of a particular social reality.

And so sending her words into this field, Germaine Greer argued that women do not want rape, had to justify her fear of a child molester as a girl with a quotation from Eldridge Cleaver, describing rape as "bloody, hateful, bitter and malignant." And my own words were bent and strained in the same way. I become tired even thinking of the labors with which I struggled with propriety and assumption in my own mind. Feeling the need to prove that rape was not an event we were bound to accept through the natural order, I pointed to cultures in which rape was a totally foreign concept; as if the fear of rape were simply a woman's paranoia, I quoted statistics which proved how often women are raped. Over and over in different ways I had to work against a mountain of argumentation that in one way or another apologized for rape, arguments that women desire rape, that rapists are victims of sexual repression, overwhelmed by bodily needs, that accusations of rape are merely projections of female fantasy. At its heart, the whole issue of rape seemed to revolve around whether or not one could trust a woman's word; and behind this questioning of our word, whether one could trust a woman's being, whether we could *trust our own being*.

And yes, studies are still being done seeking to prove that women want to be raped or cause their own rapes. Pornography, and a kind of subtle, ingrained pornographic culture surround us with images of women who seek domination, humiliation, enslavement, who take pleasure in these states. But I am no longer impassioned to argue with anyone that women do not seek pain, that we do not want to be raped; that we do not cause our own rapes. Because in this last eight years (between the writing of the first and second essays in this book), we have created another culture for ourselves— a refuge in which women's words are believed—and we can experience the truth of ourselves in words and images. This is a place of the mind, but still a place, made by bent and strained words, so that now, our words do not have to be so bent, so strained.

Now, writing from this place, I want more than the mere unmasking or naming of atrocity. I have lived in a free place, and my head is filled with different visions. I am trying to think of a world in which rape would be a foreign concept. What would that world be? How would I be different if rape never existed?

But how did we come to envision a world without rape? For to assume that such a world can exist is an amazing departure from a past we all share which told us rape was as inevitable and inalterable as rainstorms in our lives. To dream of a world without rape is to dream of indeed a radically different world.

That world of 1970 did not give birth to such dreams: so much in the way of assumption would have to be wiped away, a whole field cleared for such visions to grow. For the issue of rape was in no way ever separate from the question of the whole liberation of women as we had been defined by patriarchy, and we did not see it as separate. To begin with, for us to begin to protest against rape we had to see that there was such a thing as a patriarchy, and once seeing patriarchy, other conditions became visible to us, and other lies about these conditions. We knew that we were not the protected and thoughtless beings whom men saw in our places. We knew our own sexuality, our own feelings about motherhood, work, our spirits. We knew we would not perish without men or marriage to men, and we were capable, now, we knew, of even clearer thought than they, because we had ceased to believe the lies of sexual politics. We knew that a world without rape would be one in which we were seen for what we are, and we would grow as large in our powers as we were able.

And when I ask how did we come to envision a world without rape, I am asking about the shape of revolutions because when one dreams of a new world, this world immediately becomes possible.

II

To believe something about oneself (or of others that one has power over) is to help to make it true. There are studies which show that a teacher's expectations of a student's intelligence are usually met with the degree of intelligence expected. Hence this movement of disbelief, in which women formed a kind of mental energy wave and began to unburden ourselves of any notion that we liked suffering or oppression, was a radical act, a transforming act. Even the act of naming our suffering as oppression transformed us. The more we believed we did not like suffering, the less we found suffering, of the sort that is inflicted on one being by another, tolerable. We allowed our anger over the infliction of pain to be expressed and in that expression found more of the truth of our feelings.

I am aware that this is a classic form of knowledge, that it is the path of many therapies and healing, and also of the processes of writing and art. Creation. One allows. One follows feelings. They open and reveal deeper feeling and finally deeper meaning, and finally at some point those meanings began to transform and transmute.

This transformation moved many of us away from the political movements we had before followed. I had been a part of the student Left. From Marxism I had learned a habit of looking for social causes and observing how human nature is shaped by external condition. I named other atrocities and broke down other silences. What I learned from the movement for Black Liberation—the right to speak for oneself, the right to rage at the infliction of suffering—permeated my very soul.

But that Left had an ideology, which, beyond and in addition to its prejudice against women, did not agree with the changes we experienced. The strictly Marxist and socialist part of the left insisted that history moves only through class conflict, and since women are not a class by that definition, our efficacy as social changers became *sui generis* negligible. We were, in short, not important. This, of course, sounded like an echo to us of what we had heard all our lives.

In their rhetoric, the issue of rape, which seemed to be central to us—at the core of something which we could not fully explain, perhaps our being—was an epiphenomenon, a spin-off several generations away from the real cause, which was division of labor. And just as rape as a real and altogether too palpable phenomenon was diminished in their minds, so was it diminished in their agendas. Rape, after all, would only go away when capitalism did. The only real act hinged on the organization of labor. But this did not ease the burden which rape had put on our spirits, to organize labor.

We rejected the theory that capitalism had raped us. If they said patriarchy was just a form of capitalism, we said that capitalism was a form of patriarchy. But our departure from these old ways took place on a far deeper level than this dialogue. There were other leftist theories from which we departed, but our most serious difference was that theory had ceased to impress us as much as it had. Experience had become more important. *

In our actions we went right to the sorest wounds. The stories we heard of women who, after being raped, were hounded by the police in a kind of inquisition as if the woman had provoked the rape, created a terrible pain in us. We moved to act there, to stop the bleeding there. After numerous speak-outs were held, in which women stood up and told of having been raped, and then abused by the police and the judicial system, after giving ourselves the so desperately needed time to speak about a long hidden injury, we worked to change these more outrageous injustices inflicted on us by the very system which claimed to protect us.

Perhaps there was a wonderful logic in these moves that we did not see then. The traditional political left often calls such moves *reform*. In truth, changing the procedures of the judicial system does not stop rape. Still the logic was there, clear, brilliant with that kind of certainty that only emotional logic can have. True, rape itself is intolerable. But there are degrees of intolerability in the mind and these have to do with justice, and justice with the mind itself. Susan Sontag so accurately calls morality the realm of the imagination. And it is in the realm of the imagination that some of the greatest agonies are suffered; if I imagine myself guilty, even though I am not, I suffer as if I were.

And this precisely is the devastation that a legal system and a

---

* By this I do not mean to argue against thought or scholarship but rather to question the separation between thought, feeling and experience. Among other things, this separation ultimately leads to authoritarianism, and to the worship of certain theories for their own sake.

police procedure which questions the victim as if she were a criminal inflicts. If she accepts that indictment against herself for the violence done to her, she must feel guilt, and a guilt weighted with centuries of hatred for the bodies and sexual feelings of women. If, on the other hand, she does not accept this guilt, she suffers a sense of powerless outrage. Injustice of this order, that authority should blame the one who has been violated, can tear one apart. Especially if there is no one to hear or see this particular crime, or to affirm that injustice has taken place.

Hence a body of listeners and seers became, as part of our movement, an institution. We created rape protection centers. Women sat and listened as another woman who had just been raped told her story. *She was heard.* And this was healing of a festering wound, even to those of us who had never been raped, because such is the nature of a community or a movement. We all suffer what the others do in our minds.

And so we have centers for the care of rape victims and in many places police procedures have been changed. In other places, they are changing. (And in many places the old wrongs are repeated.) And then we moved also to change the courtroom procedures and the laws. That old practice whereby the woman who was raped was scrutinized in the courtroom, the history of her personal relationships brought in as evidence that she was not in essence rapable, was changed because of the feminist movement in many states.*

So too was the cautionary instruction of the judge removed, his direction to look at the victim's words with special suspicion, as if women are more liable to falsify, especially regarding sexual experience. And the legal requirement for corroboration in cases involving rape was also removed, so that, like a victim of robbery, or mugging, evidence from the one who was violated is all that is needed now in many courtrooms.

---

*For a more thoroughgoing discussion of the change in rape laws by one who has worked long and hard in this effort, see Camille LeGrand, "Rape and Rape Laws: Sexism in Society and Law," *California Law Review*, 1973, 919–941.

There *were* changes: the laws changed; courtroom procedures changed; police procedures changed. Still, and here we might fall under the shadow of defeat and say, nothing has really changed, and even feel somehow as I *have* felt, even if these conditions are not natural like earthquakes or tornadoes, even if rape is an un-natural occurrence, the truth is, the force of society is too great, the force of habit too deep; rape goes on despite our struggles.

For look at the statistics. (Statistics again—this is always a bad sign, a kind of failing of the heart, I think, when we need statistics, but yet bear with me.) The statistics say that from 1972 to 1976 rape has increased by 105 percent. How we ought to read this is not immediately clear. No crime involving violence to a human being has increased faster. Yes, of course, we have other consid-erations to take into account here. Perhaps the feminist movement, in removing the shame for many women in the fact of having been raped, has actually caused the increase of the number of reported rapes. Yet again, by the same logic, since this movement has also made it memorably clear that going to the police and then sitting through a trial can be a harrowing experience for a woman—almost as bad, sometimes worse than the rape itself—it could be said that fewer rapes are being reported.

We can ask a second question of the statistics though. Are there more convictions? But even if the answer to that is yes—except that it is not yes—but even if it were we still must ask again how many rapes out of the many are actually reported, and then we must ask how many rapists are caught. The statistics themselves on all these questions don't give us a very hopeful picture, but even if they did, would we believe them? The truth to us, in our daily experience, is quite different.

In Berkeley, where I live, the streets have gotten more and more dangerous. Staying in one's own house is risky. There is a man who has been raping women in this city for half a decade. Still he has not been caught, and when one hears that he has moved into one's neighborhood a kind of atmosphere of fear starts to permeate the sidewalks and the trees outside the windows. And he is not the only one. We know this from the way we have to protect ourselves; violence against women is growing, not diminishing.

The old theory would tell us this is a failure, only material change is real, reform is a compromise, believe that shadow of defeat.

But now, as equally and strongly as I know, without statistics, that violence against women continues, I also know we have not failed; we are not defeated. I do not *feel* defeated. This is what comes back upon me whenever that shadow falls of defeat, thinking we have not yet stopped rape, I do not feel defeat.

And now I search and reach for why. In the first place, I cite to you Carolyn Craven, one of many women who was raped by this man in Berkeley. She happened to be a reporter, a very well known one because a very good one. (And indeed let me say here, because later the relevance will be more clear, the fact that she was a reporter on public television had *everything* to do with a feminist movement for liberation and a black movement for liberation, both of which demanded people of our kind represented among newscasters.) And how can I tell you what it felt like to hear Carolyn Craven speak out about this rape. A kind of opening of the field. This terror, this subjection, this humiliation and torture, she said, we will not bear. I remember him, she said. I hold this man accountable. I hold this city accountable. I do not bear this act alone. We do not. We do not accept this state of being of submission and trembling and fear for our lives, of locking the door against brutality and sleeping uneasily, of our lives on edge, we do not accept this.

This in itself is such a healing. Imagine, those of you born after this movement began to make its mark, and remember, those of you who are older, what it was like before, when a reign of terror fell over the women of a city because a man was going about doing violence. Because no one then spoke out in anger and rage, no one said this is not right, this will not be. A horrible disheartening silence covered the whole affair, and each woman suffered her own fear privately and in this fear also suffered the private and unholy shame of those women who happened to be attacked. I tell you that in such an atmosphere it is truly hard to breathe.

Now, the materialist in me, and there *is* one, speaks up here and says, yes, yes, all this is true but this is not enough. No, I answer, no it is not. The whole strength and beauty of Carolyn Craven's speaking out and our speaking out is that none of us feels that the matter ends here. *We are saying the matter is intolerable.*

The change we have wrought is a change in consciousness. The actual condition of rape continues, as do all the conditions of women's lives which cannot be separated from rape. Through manifested acts, woven inextricably into the dominant culture, the idea of woman as a diminished being still rings through patriarchal society. She who must work longer hours and harder for less, she who is beaten and hounded by her husband into fear and hiding, she whose body is tortured in the public imagination in the name of pleasure, she who has no power in her own government, whose voice is rarely heard—this is the being who is still raped.

The atrocities continue, and we have not yet even named them all. Only two years ago, in 1976, the first International Tribunal of Crimes Against Women was held. Forced sterilization, clitoridectomy, denial of birth control, persecution of lesbians, brutality toward women giving birth, economic exploitation, these continue all over the world. And yet the conference began with these words, not defeated words, but words of overcoming, of movement.

Strengthened by your solidarity, you will develop defensive tactics, the first being precisely the one you will be using during these five days: talk to one another, talk to the world, bring to light the shameful truths that half of humanity is trying to cover up. The Tribunal is in itself a feat. It heralds more to come.

In itself a feat. It heralds more to come. I want to mine these words which Simone de Beauvoir sent to the tribunal, to find meanings perhaps even past what they were intended to mean, because this is where we are now, in time. This is what we have.

Yes, we do not yet have the end of rape. All we have is the feat of naming rape a crime against us. But how could changing police procedures and law bring an end to the raping of women? We have just said that rape is not isolated from the whole condition of women which remains a diminished condition (except now in our minds). The miseducation of young girl children, the complacency with which mutilating operations on female bodies are accepted, the poverty of women and children, that any woman anywhere feels she is not beautiful or is too old or is not fully human—all of these cause rape. They cause this act slowly, and through subtle turnings, but still certainly and predictably. When we confront rape, suddenly a whole system becomes visible, a system which includes invisibility and silence, which had covered the crime of rape in silence, and of which silencing and the ignorance of our history of protesting our condition has been an active part. So it follows that rape does not end with the changing of laws; that the causes go deeper and belong to the whole fabric.

And did we ever believe in the first place that these little changes would take away the whole crime? Did we, for instance, have a Grand Plan, in which the changing of laws or setting up of centers for the protection of women was simply a First Step? A part of a program? No. Our decision to set up places where women could be looked after by other women was not made out of revolutionary theory. In all our acts, there has been a voice heralding more to come. This is a passionate voice, a voice which has given to our small, seemingly hardly significant changes an excitement, a joy, beyond what rationally one might consider belongs. But this voice did not proceed from theory. This was a voice intrinsic to and birthed from what we did. And what we did was always, and still is, to heal ourselves.

We did not move from theory; we moved quite simply, as I wrote before, to the sorest wounds, and in this sense, we were no longer "thinking" in the way that Western man thinks, in the realm where thought is divided from feeling, and objectivity is imagined to exist. We were discovering a different sense of clarity, one achieved through feeling, in which thought followed a direction determined by pain, and trauma, and compassion and outrage. This is why we made these places where women who had been brutalized might be cared for.

Yet these small changes in the doing of things were in themselves a feat. And they do herald more to come. Because the making of these small changes changed us. And these changes inside us were not small; we were profoundly different now than we had been before.

There is an old trick known by doctors of the mind and even some of the body, and most nurses, and certainly any woman who has had the care of the ailing. Any little change for the better is liable to start a whole process in motion, and especially if that change is begun by the patient herself. Belief that one is getting well is in itself curative for the ill. To comb one's hair, brush one's teeth, stretch, to attend to even the most irrelevant detail can cause a more essential turning, go into cells themselves it seems, wake up in the body a desire to breathe. No textbook, no objective medical analysis, can tell what that detail might be which releases. An old, accomplished nurse often has hands which know to guide her patient to her own resources. This kind of knowledge is called intuitive and it is called feminine.

There is a saying which is part of Oriental medicine and that is that Ki, or energy, or the life force, follows mind. Placing one's mind and heart in a certain direction, believing, can make it so. Certainly many women found this to be true when they learned to defend themselves. Much of the study of martial arts, besides the physical development of grace and skill, is a change in attitude. To work against fear, shock, a feeling of defeat. To use the energy of the attacker against himself. And this change in attitude brings about a change in the material. The body becomes stronger, quicker, gravitates to the physical, seeks movement; and the body which feels strong, which feels it can defend itself affects the mind, cannot be seized in the same way by fear, transforms the psyche.

In this way, no change we experienced was simply itself but made other changes. And the shape of each change became a lesson for us in possibility.

We did not lack sophistication. We knew we were supposed to have theories. Indeed, the presence of this goal, to change the whole order of things, was an issue among us. We lived in a mood of vigilance and still do that our movement not end in a series of ameliorating social services.

We were not satisfied that women had gotten the vote, just as we knew the women with vision in the nineteenth and early twentieth century who had struggled for that vote had not intended for the matter to end with that accomplishment. We would not be satisfied if the centers we invented for the caring of women who had been raped got sucked up into officialdom, standardized, bureaucratized. In this, what we were doing would be lost as surely as certain artifacts, certain sacred objects, lose their meaning utterly in even the most careful replicas.

What was it in what we did that could not be replicated by this social order we try to see ourselves past? On a very practical level, we went about things differently than they are usually done. Writing of the parallel movement to set up women's health care centers, a woman in Switzerland warns, "They must not become imitations of already established institutions by, for instance, being seduced by profit, having a hierarchy of salaries and workers, and by practicing established medicine."

Really, what happened that was so radically changing for so many of us, was that, as we began to create our own places (and this includes places of the mind), everything fell under question. None of the old ways of thinking and doing were assumed to be right.

This was not an easy way of being. We struggled among each other, sometimes gloomily. We had to discover that creating our own lives was not an answer in itself, but only a beginning. Paradise is not conferred on the liberated. We became free in these places of our own creation only to see troubles and failures of our own making.

But our failures have been pale beside what we have wrought within ourselves. Can we begin to see this now when the future to so many seems portentous with violence and scarcity?

Helen Marieskind, writing of the self-help clinic movement says,

The self-help clinic and the women's health movement are not just personal solutions for an individual women's health problem—though that is obviously a valid reason for their existence: they are tools for inducing collective thought and action from which radical social change can grow.

But let us look closely at these words. To begin with, to say that a clinic might validly exist as a solution for an individual woman's health problem is a radical statement! If women are suffering in our bodies, this suffering should be met. This suffering should not be tolerated. Most really revolutionary change seems, after the fact, to be self-evident. That all children should be educated. That workers ought to receive enough pay for a decent standard of living. That it should be a crime to enslave another human being. These are all self-evident to us, but what a labor it was to bring this evidence before a self which civilization had damaged and contorted into thinking otherwise.

In assuming that women's bodies ought to be cared for we are pushing aside centuries of hatred for the female body. Of the malignment of women's complaints. We are challenging the belief that women ought to suffer, that physical pain is a part of our destiny and ill health a part of our biology.

But Helen Marieskind's sentence goes on and becomes more radical. She speaks of that motion where the patient begins to care for herself. These are our health care centers. We are directing the motions. We have initiated their very existence.

One must know the history of women and medicine to comprehend the depth of this change, and it is part of this feminist movement, part of the heralding more to come, that we have revived this history. I cannot tell the whole story here. A few details will have to suffice. For instance, the fact that midwives, who had been delivering infants successfully for centuries were stopped from practicing by patriarchal law. That the women burned as witches were often herbal healers if not midwives. That women were denied entrance for centuries into medical colleges. And that those who gained knowledge otherwise were refused the license which would allow them to practice. The most powerfully affirming act, to heal oneself, or, in the imagination to see oneself as having the power of healing because one knows that is part of being human which is being female, this is what has been denied us. And this and no less than this is what we have taken back when we have created health centers and centers for the care of women who have been raped.

Finally Marieskind says that these movements induce "collective thought and action from which radical change can grow." But how could they not? When one takes one's own healing which is to take one's own life into one's own hands, how can this not change our behavior and how we think and how we feel? *In itself a feat. It heralds more to come.* Healing, and the belief we can heal ourselves, and desire to heal and the decision to move toward healing are all radical acts which transform us in and of themselves. Once so transformed by these seemingly small acts, we are capable of vision, of imagination and more decisions and more actions, because by the process of caring for ourselves, we become more and more ourselves.

A woman is raped. A rape is attempted on a small girl. A woman reads about a rape in the newspaper. This woman does not report the rape to the police because the man who raped her was once a lover. The little girl is questioned rigorously by a policeman who wants to know if she makes up stories. The woman reading the newspaper sees the word *alleged* appear again and again in front of the word *rape*.

What would happen if these two women and the little girl met, if they spoke, if they were able to speak out what they felt to each other? What would happen if they discovered the same rape, the same hurt, the same feeling of being distrusted, perhaps turned into distrust of the self, suffocation from buried feeling, the same relief at finally knowing that what they knew to be true both in their own souls and in the world outside them was true. What happens when thinking and feeling beings begin to trust themselves, their own perceptions, *their own desires even?* What happens when we follow what we feel, do what we desire? If one woman holds another after she has been raped. Stays with her through the night. Listens to her story. If a group of women demand that a judge not caution his jury to distrust the words of women. Doesn't this same miracle happen when a woman knows, because her hands themselves have discovered this, that she can care for her own body, that she may know more than the doctor knows, because she feels. These are kinds of healing, to restore sight and hearing, to restore voice and movement, all through belief, because through these experiences, we believe ourselves again and therefore, we become ourselves as never before.

These new beings which we always were but had been separated from, these new souls never settle for the old ways which had buried them. And these souls can suddenly imagine more than rape centers, or laws changed, or even prisons full of men who have raped women. These souls, because they have had a taste of being whole, a taste of wellness, begin to desire even more. Now we desire a world in which rape could not be imagined and could never be. We desire nothing less than this.

What I have described here is a new shape for revolutions, though perhaps this is the way deep change has always occurred. Because the beginning is in feeling, and one follows the heart, not the head. After all, our heads have been schooled in the old way of doing things, whether we call that way patriarchy or capitalism or tradition or the establishment, this is how we have been schooled. The right way of doing things. The way it has always been done. What the authorities say should happen, whether those authorities be Keynes or Marx or Weber or St. Paul.

About four years ago, I had a dream which was set at a radical political convention. I found a group of people whose ideas charmed me. I found myself sympathetic and began to march with them until I asked them their name. They said they were Trotskyists. What faction they were, in the dream, did not bother me. However, I was horrified to learn that they had named themselves after one man. My dream soul found this the height of absurdity, and I began to laugh in astonishment.

What we are schooled to believe ought to happen is always a rigidity, a limitation on what can be. As a poet, I have known this for years. When I begin to write, if I have in my head a notion of what the poem must be, the poem is always curiously, sadly, small and predictable. But if I follow the words which come from my feeling, often times not even knowing quite what they mean, certainly not guessing the outcome, I find the poem becoming wondrously large. My own words become a kind of gift to me.

Must not a real revolution transform even the expectations of the revolutionaries? And must it not therefore proceed, with all sureness, from the heart?

III

Look at the skeleton children
advancing against us
beneath their faces there is no sunlight
no darkness
no heart remains
no legends
to bring them back as women
into their bodies at dawn.
                —Audre Lorde, "Chain"

Whatever divided us from our own hearts so that we should even have to speak of such a thing as moving from our hearts, as if this were not natural? Where is it we have been? What strange life have we been living? These are the questions I awaken with in 1978. I find myself remaking myself each day, learning like a small child such simple things as where is the earth, where is the sky, what does my body feel like, how can I let my own weight give me grace, how do I speak directly, see, what does the world tell me, from moment to moment. Because I have been a damaged being, as we are all damaged. The real sources of my own power and knowledge were taken from me painfully, slowly and surely, as a child, as we were all so maimed in our sense of the real.

I discovered my rage and fear at the existence of rape. And beyond this? Solitude. Myself. What am I if I exist unprotected in the world? These are beginning to be questions for the soul, and these are the questions, after seven years of political questioning, which like the kernel of wheat after it has been held up to the wind, remain. But is this not what we have meant all along when we have demanded to be human?

And yet, we who were the objects, the "other," less than human, have found in our struggle to free ourselves from this less-than-whole definition which patriarchy lent to us, that no one in the patriarchy is fully human, that even what is called human in that world of dominance is sadly, deeply diminished.

Look what we discovered in our political motions to liberate ourselves from the terror of rape. We found all acts of transformation transform us. That we must follow our feelings; that we can heal ourselves; that we find the unexpected. But these are all words that concern the spirit, and yet the spirit has either a corrupted place in patriarchal politics, or no place at all.

In 1971, when I wrote the first part of this work, I considered the spiritual movement to be a digression, an escape from the real causes of human suffering. This was an attitude I had inherited from the Left, and which was natural to me at that time, since what I had known of the spiritual was mostly a hypocritical wielding of symbols in the use of power. As Nelle Morton has written of the official sanctity,

> The Lordship of Christ often becomes strangely identified with earthly lords and rulers who supply funds for certain religious groups to exist, invite its leaders to the White House, and use them to bless proceedings in courts and legislative assemblies.

When the spiritual was not divided from the political this seemed a sinister, almost sickening encroachment on liberty. And Marx's words that "all progress of the spirit had thus far been progress against the mass of mankind, driving it into an ever more dehumanized situation," seemed manifestly true, not only in the history of the atrocities of the crusades and the missionaries, but also in the history of the oppression of women, the burning of witches, and the long and virulent tradition of the hatred of women by the Church Fathers which supported those burnings and lived long after. In my own life, I ascribed many kinds of suffering, both in the body and the mind, to Christian ideas which had become part of me.

And yet in 1978 I find myself speaking with my own soul. And so I want to go back, further back into the reaches of the past and know where or how what was called spiritual became a way through which we were even further alienated from ourselves. Because now the old patriarchal habit of dividing one thing from another—matter from spirit, body from soul, the left hand from the right, the one from the other—no longer works for me, and I, together with many women in this continuing movement into our lives, find that things spiritual and things political are no longer separate.

I am trying in these pages, to tell how this happened. But this is not easy. I grope; the language is not available. What is here is old language with old connotations. Even the words *soul* and *spirit* have become so corrupted, so removed from immediate experience, mystified, used as mystification, as a way to alienate a being from herself. So I must just string together a series of simple stories and observations and hope this way we will find some thread of meaning.

First, I go back again to the matter of consciousness, consciousness which has become so significant to the feminist, and was so diminished for the Marxist. But in this there is a wonderful paradox. It was a Marxist education which in the first place made me distrust all theory and give experience primacy. But this is what led me, and all of us I believe, to consciousness and then to the soul—because we were more vitally interested in our own experience than theory. Where our experience contradicted traditional radical thought, we left that thought behind. And in our very living, in our paying attention to our real lives, we encountered the crucial fact of the significance of our minds, in no experience more dramatically than in the experience of rape.

In their statement against rape delivered at the International Tribunal on Crimes Against Women, a group of French women said this:

Legally, rape is recognized as a crime with physical aspects only; namely the penetration of the vagina by the penis against the will of the victim. In effect however, the real crime is the annihilation by the man of the woman as a human being.

One physical act is not equal to another physical act. Rape is not a matter of spiritless atoms penetrating other dead matter. Mind comes to play. Will comes to play. The act is informed by centuries of the hatred of women, by a tradition of violence and fear toward our bodies, by St. Paul's words that we ought to keep silent, by the old rule that we must cover our heads in church. This is what makes rape a qualitatively different act than assault, or robbery. In both cases, one is forced, one is injured. But in the case of rape, the very odor of the body of the rapist, his gestures of brutality, the menace of his threats echo back into centuries of debasement and his penetration penetrates the very soul of his victim with, as the French women wrote, annihilation.

But isn't the thought that women have no soul one of the preconditions of rape, and is not rape, after all, a ritualistic playing out of that belief? Two monks in the fourteenth century wrote that women are not to be trusted in the realm of the spiritual, that this is why they are more open to possession by the devil. After the death by suicide of a film actress, another actress publicly declares, "They treat us like meat," by which she means that the men who hire them treat them as less than human, as matter without spirit. A young man who has committed a rape confesses that, as he forced this young woman, a stranger to him, her cries of fear made him realize suddenly, as if this had never before occurred to him, that she was a human being.

This is perhaps the most mutilating of dichotomies in these centuries, that some are seen as fully human and some are not. Simone de Beauvoir has written about us,

Now, what peculiarly signalizes the situation of woman is that she—a free and autonomous being like all human creatures—nevertheless finds herself living in a world where men compel her to assume the status of the other.

This is also true of people of color, of homosexuals. The Other takes many shapes. And the mutilation which occurs in this act of consciousness through which the soul of the Other is stolen, is a mutilation which cuts both ways. For certainly it is mutilating to deprive the Other of a soul, and beyond a doubt it is mutilating to rape. No wonder indeed that the spirit has a doubtful life in the patriarchy.

But this may be the reason, finally, that our very selfish motion, to heal ourselves, to tend to our own wounds, may turn out to be the most radical motion of all, one that heals not only ourselves but eventually all, and thus transforms the social order absolutely. For indeed, the rapist does not feel the agony of rape; the nature of his particular mutilation is a numbing. To fail to see the soul of another is to truncate perception utterly. But the one who is raped cannot rest still with her situation. She is turned on a rack, herself and her own body put in direct opposition to the state of the world as society has asked her to accept it. Of this de Beauvoir writes,

The drama of woman lies in this conflict between the fundamental aspirations of every subject (ego)—who always regards the self as the essential—and the compulsions of a situation in which she is inessential.

How could a woman be more quintessentially inessential except when she is being raped? Her very life is under threat of extinction. The dictates of her soul are rendered without effect. And any sense of being essential in this context must therefore be an extremity, an act which strikes at the core of patriarchy. Isn't this the reason why under the law it has been so much more acceptable for a man to strike out against the rapist of his wife or his daughter than it is for the woman herself to do so? Behind the letter of the law is a reasoning based on property rights, so that even here the crime of rape is not a crime against an inessential being but against her owner, the essential being who is her husband or her father.

Was not this the real question behind the trials of Inez Garcia, Joanne Little, Yvonne Wanrow, and now Dessie Woods?* And how significant really that these four women are all defined as the inessential Other in two ways, both as women and as women who are of another race. How can the Other have the basically human right to defend herself against violence? Her life is not essential.

Indeed, to find in ourselves that quality of being essential is no small task. This process does not stop with eliminating shame at being raped, though this is a beginning. We must strip ourselves to the very core, strip away all the patriarchal learning, the old alienating definition of soul as not female. I find it significant that Inez Garcia decided to protest her case publicly when she heard of the rape of two girl children. When my daughter was born, I suddenly felt a new level of rage at what had been done to women, what is done to us, from birth. It is as if we must somehow be able to imagine ourselves as innocent and new born again if we are to reach within ourselves our own essentialness.

And essence, after all, is another word for soul, is another word for spirit—the spirit which is lost to the rapist and the raped, in this transgression. And so there is a shape here after all, moving from the political to the spiritual.

But there is more. The motion has even more of a shape, winds in more intricate patterns, yields more details. There are other stories. Because the stripping away which one must do in this patriarchy to retrieve oneself goes on in many ways. And one of them was in the realm of traditional religion itself. For alongside protests against rape and the poverty of women and the many material ways

---

*Each of these women was put on trial for murder because they killed the men who raped them or, in the case of Yvonne Wanrow, also threatened her children.

of our brutalization, steadily, over these last seven years, women have been retrieving what was lost to us in culture. There were a multitude of starting points. The use of the word *human* to mean "male." The use of the term *him* to mean "her" and "him", but still always really "him". All the books by women fallen out of print, not taught to us in school; paintings by women stored away in museums; female mythology subtly changed over centuries so that what was female became male and the very features by which we recognize the heroic became masculine. That God is male. All the ways our presence has been erased from the mirror of culture. Another aspect of our non-being.

And so we began to reprieve pictures of ourselves. We wrote, sang, painted. We recovered the writings and markings of women who lived before. We scrutinized all the old stories and images handed down to us so that we might gaze directly on the hatred of women in these tales. The story of Lilith. The story of Eve. The paintings of Salome and of the Madonna. And in all this we found two amazing revelations which may be keys to this rejoining of the spiritual and the political I attempt here.

One of these revelations was that the patriarchal religion was not only incidentally misogynist but that hatred of the female (and with that the uncontrolled, the emotional, the intuitive, the dark, the world) is woven so inextricably into these religions that one might say this is *the* hidden content of, for instance, Christianity. And at the same time we discovered another revelation: that there were, at different times in history, different religions and mythologies which worshipped female gods.

To place before one's mind the image of a Goddess. Not the goddess as consort or mother or younger sister, but as the powerful one, the source, the revealer of mystery: If a woman is to become essential, must not this image be a possibility for her?

And then, of course, the actual shape of history began to suggest more. Nothing could be proven absolutely. What we had, what we have, are suggestions. But that is all we need. We remake the past in our minds, for now that is all the past is for us anyway—a place in our minds which has its greatest power in perhaps determining for us what we can imagine as the future.

We received the suggestion that those women who were burned by the Christian Fathers as witches were indeed the priestesses of a different religion, one which was more female not only in its offices, but in the more transcendent meanings of the word female: closer to the earth, listening to natural spirits, emotional, sexual, dark. We recovered images from prehistory. Rounded female Goddesses, found buried in fields, left from older civilizations. A Goddess with snakes as symbols of power wound about her arms. The sacred calf. The tree of life. The symbols which the patriarchal religion had called evil.

And indeed we found that in this mythological world the story of rape was told with great clarity. That the sites of matriarchal temples, such as Knossos on Crete, were chosen because the surrounding hills made the shape of a female body. That a female deity preceded Zeus. That Zeus raped Hera. And then we listened with new ears to the story of the rape of Persephone—how the daughter was stolen from her mother, how she was raped with her father's blessings, how her mother made the earth unyielding in revenge and received her daughter back only by compromise.

All this knowledge worked a kind of alchemy in us which cannot easily be described by rational means. Can I say simply that a woman who can perceive in herself the Goddess cannot so easily be shamed by rape? That she is more likely to shame her rapist? For we are not protesting anymore that we too are human. We are not bent and strained to argue that we do not want rape, eager to prove that rape is a crime. We take our essentialness as self-evident now, and our work begins with this. So we begin to see, and we see differently. We see what is not there. We see visions. We know there *is* a world without rape and this world is in our minds.

IV

When you have buried us   told your story
our does not end   we stream

into the unfinished   the unbegun
the possible
—Adrienne Rich, "Phantasia For Elvira Shatayev"

We are essential. We are translucent to ourselves. We have taken the power outside us within us. We have stripped away the voice of the authority. We become our own authority. We are the only ones who can say if we have souls, and we say we do, and these souls speak to us. Our conversations with the spirit are our own. No one else translates, or listens in, or can tell us what has transpired. What we know we know. We speak directly to the spirit.

And was this not Anne Hutchinson's crime? In the sixteenth century Anne Hutchinson was banished from the Massachusetts Bay Colony because she preached, and because of *what* she preached. In trial, when she asked why she should not preach, Governor Winthrop and the elders of Boston quoted to her the words of St. Paul, "I permit not a woman to teach." When the Other stands up and acts as if she is essential, this act by itself challenges the existing order.

And yet again, Anne Hutchinson, having had the experience of the Other, must have had that consciousness, undergone that old stripping away somewhere in herself, redefined the world, been born as new outside the old definitions. What she preached tells us this must have been so. Even in the angry and condemning words of Governor Winthrop the luminescence of her vision comes through. She taught, he reports, a covenant of grace as opposed to a covenant of works. What grace meant in that time and ethos and that community was that one knew God only directly through an immediate revelation of the spirit, and could not be said to be saved because of regular church attendance, or wealth, * or any baptisms conferred

---

* From a materialist point of view, or to one concerned with circumstances and social conditions, belief in the covenant of grace might appear to be a reactionary theology, since participation in the mystery of grace does not necessitate any outwardly caring behavior toward others in order to achieve salvation. Yet in the context of seventeenth-century politics the covenant of good works was in fact the more conservative theology, since it ultimately bolstered both the authority of the church and the Protestant work ethic. In its more developed and extreme form,

by earthly authorities. This idea clearly moved Winthrop to terror. He wrote, "Many good soules, that had been of long approved godlinesse were brought to renounce all the work of grace in them, and wait for this immediate revelation."

But how exciting these words sound to me. How much I desire that "long approved godlinesse" should be thoroughly renounced in me. How I value this "immediate revelation" for which I wait, and which I receive, and for which I wait again daily. And yet how dangerous is this idea, this theology in which the soul speaks directly to the soul and her universe.

And have we not then, in the stripping away of the voices of patriarchal authority from our minds in order to make ourselves essential once again, established for ourselves a direct relation with our own hearts, our spirit which is the same as the universe, the spirit?

Consider just this. This same voice of patriarchal authority which declared that women desire pain and ought to cover our heads in church is that which eventually separated things political from things spiritual, matter from soul, and declared all that was not material as unreal. Science now replaces the Church Fathers with its own religion of atheism. Patriarchy has judged its own god as dead. And this is most certainly true. Those who rape have murdered their own souls. But we who have been the raped are not enclosed in this system. We are inessential only to it. Not to ourselves. And our souls then, once we step outside of this enclosure, are not dead. Neither is the spirit of the world, we can see now, dead.

Knowing this, should it be a surprise that the feminist movement

---

this covenant acted as an apologia for the rich; wealth was said to be a sign of internal holiness. Of the question of caring, I remind myself that Anne Hutchinson was a healer (she was a midwife). And to this apparent contradiction I bring the Buddhist idea of compassion, that is, of a spontaneous act of warmth which because it is creative, is also propitious and deeply kind, but which never springs from the calculated desire to be charitable, "good," or religously correct. I imagine a true state of grace would generate this kind of compassion. And here too I remember these lines from H.D.'s "The Flowering of the Rod," "I go to the things I love with no thought of duty or pity."

has led many of us to speak directly, and now I am being concrete and particular, with spirits. I myself have found a new way of being in this world.

I know that hands find the places on the body which need touching. Certain places have become sacred for me, as if the trees there have held part of my soul and know me. A light falls around the body, a light that can touch and be touched and flows from one being to another. One tree grieves for me when I am sad and is glad to see me when I visit. The day I suddenly wanted so deeply to resolve a long bitterness with an old friend that I saw her clearly in my mind's eye, she appeared a few moments later before me in the flesh. And deer come to me and linger at those particular moments when my own nature seems to crack and open to me so that I speak directly with the universe. I call to an old friend who is dead; I say, give me a sign of your presence and in the next block her name appears over a storefront I have never seen before. I stare into the mirror at the bones of my face, I stare into the charred hollow of a tree trunk, at another woman's hands. I touch the skull of a deer, touch the place between my breasts. Around the objects carved and revered by Eskimos, I can feel a presence. After playing music here I begin to feel a presence in the air outside my kitchen. Because I share a kind of bread with a friend in love, this bread is forever filled with her, evokes tenderness in me, comforts me. Gradually my whole landscape *is* touched, is sacred. Day by day I shed the old rational apparatus. I become more and more alienated from the assumed way of thinking and doing, but—and this is the miracle which keeps me in this direction—I become more and more myself, less and less alienated from that self for whom, more and more, I feel a great love.

Can I say here how wild I feel? That the visions in my mind are as real as this manifested vision of the patriarchy whose streets I must negotiate every day. How is it I can let you know that this is becoming daily more true for other women all over the country. And that we find new powers in ourselves. New ways of hearing and seeing and healing. That we begin to feel a kinship with the ways people thought and think in tribes, in Indian cultures. That we feel the universe speaks to us, cares for us, leads us. That what we experience directly from the universe finally has more power for us than what all the authorities of "approved godlinesse"—the doctors, the scientists, the Academies—have taught us.

This then is how finally, in 1978 when I turn to write about rape, I decide to write about how this violence impinges on a woman's spiritual life. In the nineteenth century Susan B. Anthony, the political leader, and Annie Besant, the spiritual leader, could not agree. They thought their worlds, the spiritual and the political, to be separate. Now we erase this old, damaging separation. Now women all over speak of the spirit in political language, of the political through the words of the spirit. Mary Daly, once a Catholic theologian, creates an image of what has been called God— this being at the heart of things—which cannot be a noun, must be a verb, a process, a becoming, our becoming. Nelle Morton, another feminist, imagines "a great ear at the heart of the universe hearing human beings to speech—to new creation. A speech that is human speech—human word—my word and your word. Our word become flesh."

Our word become flesh. We are inside ourselves. We have felt ourselves as never before. I tell you this and offer no evidence except the words on the page because no evidence of such an experience can be given. Except to know that we are learning to love the essence in ourselves, and thus we learn to love each other in ways before unimaginable.

V

Now we are ready
and each of us knows it   I have never loved
like this   I have never seen
my own forces so taken up and shared
and given back

After the long training   the early sieges
we are moving almost effortlessly in our love
                    —Adrienne Rich, "Phantasia for Elvira Shatayev"

1978. I go deep into myself. I suffer the pains of the past which I know I have always carried with me. I see that what I saw before as real was delusion. Every motion I make to heal myself widens my vision. This comes upon me as joy, as an experience of gladness, that the world can be what I imagine. Rape is an invention. Rape can be unimaginable. I feel this is my very flesh, this flesh which opens to joy. I feel safety. I know what this state is. I feel blessedness. I say we can pronounce this world differently. Our word can become, flesh.

VI

1985. Seven years have passed. The violence that has increased over a decade stays the same now, neither increasing nor diminishing. The pitch and frequency of threat and attack are high. And in this atmosphere we conduct our daily lives. This has been a difficult year. In the spring my close friend Elissa died. The day is hot. The sun makes everything glitter.

Unexpectedly the door bell rings. I do not know the woman who stands there. She tells me she has recently moved into the neighborhood, and the other night two men tried to rape her. I can see the fear in her body as she speaks. I go to tell Claire who lives downstairs. Grief over the death of our mutual friend has made us close. I watch the fear I saw in my neighbor's body enter her body. It is as if a weight were placed on her back. As she hunches over, the space between us starts to contract.

In the newspaper I read a study. Women who have been raped suffer for a long time afterward. There are phobias, there are sleepless nights, flashbacks. One of the doctors who conducted this study says she believes these difficulties continue because the women who were attacked thought they would be killed.

Then in Thomas Merton's essay on Gandhi, I encounter a word I have not heard before, and this word begins to repeat itself in my mind like a chant: *satyagraha*, it promises to shed some new light on the subject of rape; *satyagraha*, this word created by Gandhi for an ancient way of being—holding onto the truth; *satyagraha*, not simply facts but a deeper wisdom that informs the body, the soul, and shapes further action.

It strikes me now that one of the untold burdens of the survivor of rape is what she has come to know. She has been left holding the truth. It is not only a threat of death she has encountered. That threat has carried with it a malevolence and an insanity with a long history. Before she is raped a woman may know statistics about the frequency of rape, and the atmosphere of violence cannot have escaped her. She, like other women, will have been careful at night. Perhaps she has even avoided going out alone after dark. But now, after being raped, the look of daily life is imbued with this event. Terror lies at the edge of the simplest habits. For her the world has changed. And in this understanding she is isolated, because for us who have not been raped the world remains the same. We keep the fact of rape at the periphery of consciousness and do not let it bear on our vision.

There is a politics of consciousness which determines what we will allow ourselves to know and how deeply we will hold the truth. In the past seven years, the movement for the liberation of women has brought to public consciousness two phenomena, one a kind of rape and another a cause of rape: the sexual abuse of children and pornography. In the same years we have become more aware of the increasing danger of nuclear war. And this is no coincidence. Rape and warfare are part of one civilization, part of a weave of thought, behavior, institution. Were we to allow them to speak to us, the images of pornography and the testimony of those who survive rape would bear not only on our understanding of sexual violence but on the question of war too.

In one instant a whole city is destroyed. A child dies. His mother is ill for the rest of her life with radiation poisoning. A woman is attacked, her vagina torn so that it will not heal. Her life is filled with an uneasy fear. Because in the shape of a single life these events seem utterly without any purpose, there is at the core of this kind of suffering a profound feeling of senselessness. And yet suffering can be used. The knowledge of the survivor can be given, passed on from one generation to another, spread through wider and wider circles.

The survivor of Hiroshima has a knowledge essential to our survival in this century. And so does the survivor of rape. She has encountered the secret madness of our civilization, the sexual dimension of violence. And she has learned the toll that this insanity exacts on the body. *Satyagraha.* Where does destruction hide in our ideas of the masculine and the feminine, in our ideas of who we are? It is not a partial truth that we need to hold, but the whole of truth.

What is the whole truth? From a human perspective, which is the only one possible for us, we can never know the whole truth. But there are certain truths that we each experience. We can choose either to recognize or deny what we see or feel. In this sense, at any given moment, a life can be lived truthfully or not.

In a small town in Minnesota a child disappears. As word spreads that she is missing, neighbors organize a search party. They bring meals for the child's mother and father. Seven weeks later her body is found. In the wake of mourning, a group is formed to help missing children, and the dead girl's father is chosen as the leader of this group. And then after the police question him, her father confesses. He had been assaulting her for five years. She had begun to resist. He drove her to the countryside and when she fought, he stabbed her and watched as she bled to death. When news of this reaches the town, its citizens find it unfathomable. This was a hard-working man. He took his children fishing and swimming. Even he himself appears to have trouble knowing what he did. For a long time he cannot clearly remember if he murdered his daughter or not. Among his friends and neighbors some understanding begins to grow that such an event can happen in this place, a small town in rural America.

There is a sense in which the feminist movement has steadily widened the aperture of consciousness. Piece by piece we construct a new picture of who we are. First we acknowledge that rape occurs frequently and affects the lives of all women. Then we begin to see how often children are raped, and that they are raped by those they trust and love—fathers, uncles, brothers, teachers.

But like the residents of a small town who have been forced to acknowledge violence, we are still in a state of shock. This is not who we thought we were. And we hold the truth only fleetingly, like images from a dream, dimly recalled, half-remembered, growing vague, eluding the comprehension that would lead to change. Our solutions are partial.

I think for instance of the policy of certain social service agencies which determines that after a child has been raped by her father, every attempt will be made to reunite the family and thus send the child back into the home to live again with the father who raped her.

One does not know how to respond to such a solution. Can a man who rapes his daughter be so easily, so quickly changed? One attempts to imagine the point of view of the child. Even if all traces of the old behavior are gone from her father, the child may not be free of her fear. And one suspects that the child may carry a fear so deep and so habitual that she cannot even speak it. As if she had had a long illness and forgotten what it is to be well, she has forgotten what it is to feel safe.

Yet, as much as this solution has the feeling of a nightmare in which the same attacker appears at every exit, this is a predictable ending. We have all been shaped to expect it. We share a way of thinking with the social service agency. We are not surprised to hear that the goal of this policy is to preserve the family. What we have allowed ourselves to hear in the testimony of the survivor has been siphoned through a grid of already determined meanings. The full impact of what we hear fails to reach us, and so many implications escape us.

In a recent article Florence Rush writes that she would not have believed the problem of the sexual abuse of children could receive so much attention and yet at the same time be so little changed. She attributes this to the quality of our understanding. We have forgotten the history of sexual abuse. Small girls bartered into marriage. Rape only a violation in the sense that a father's or a husband's property rights are violated. We tell ourselves the rape of children is a modern problem. That this form of abuse was before veiled in silence and is now spoken of everywhere only tends to support this illusion. Not remembering, or never learning history, we can believe that rape is just one more result of abandoning civilization's fundamental values. That rape and the sexual abuse of children actually proceeds from those values and from the very institutions we see as "normal" remains inconceivable.

From many sources—the testimony of his patients, medical reports, autopsies, even books by other doctors—Sigmund Freud received evidence of the wide frequency of the sexual abuse of children. For a short period he believed the evidence that came to him, and then he changed his mind and developed the theory that children have fantasies of being raped by their parents.* Had he held onto the truth he at first perceived he would have had to question the very roots of his own thinking about men and women

---

*see Florence Rush, *The Best Kept Secret*, 1980; Alice Miller, *Thou Shalt Not Be Aware*, 1983; Jeffrey Moussaieff Masson, *The Assault on Truth*, 1984.

and the family. Above all, he had the kind of mind that integrates knowledge with other knowledge so that seemingly disparate details fall into one picture. Many of the values Freud most cherished might have collapsed under the weight of his own scrutiny had he admitted the truth of what we now know to be true.

It is frequently the claim of those empowered by a particular social system that the system of thought—version of history, way of seeing—that supports that system is objective. As Bishop Tutu writes of the official white history of South Africa, "We heard a great deal about Western historical objectivity; it all seemed to suggest that Western historians were able to describe the naked, the real facts without any kind of embellishment or accretion, that they were quite uninfluenced by who they were and where they were, able, as it were, to stand outside themselves. . . ."

Often a particular system of thought will have as its purpose not only to reveal certain truths but also to conceal others. In this way what appears to be perfectly logical within that system seems like madness outside of it. Within the military system of thought, it is a sane and logical conclusion that the way to prevent nuclear war is to stockpile nuclear weapons.

Because conventional thought on the subject of rape poses itself as objective, one is always trying to argue with it. But objective truth, that is, truth from no perspective at all, does not exist. I am trying to move away from the prose of argument to shape a language in speaking of rape, that allows for openings in the old system of thought, without staying in a fixed dialogue with that thought.

I think of the writer Theresa Hak Kyung Cha. A few years ago I found a copy of her book, *Dictee*. The form and language of this book are entirely experimental. Playing with different styles—the historical style, the style of correspondence, of official documents— and lifting them out of their usual contexts, she constantly makes us see past our habitual ways of seeing events. From the bookseller I learned that this writer died recently. She was attacked and murdered on a city street.

In her book she wrote about a history that has been lost, the history of Korea. Of Korea invaded by Japan. Of her mother, an immigrant from Korea. Of the process of speech. *I am composing. Recording movements. You are here I raise the voice. Particles of sound and noise gathered pick up lint, dust. They might scatter and become invisible.* These were her words. Now she has become invisible.

I want to take in each of these truths. This woman has died. Her death was senseless. She died by violence. This violence is directed at all women, at our sexuality. Her book breaks the old forms. In her writing, she speaks of what it is to be a woman and a Korean. She speaks of an unknown history. Her book has passed into print with almost no recognition, like the books of many other women, or the books of those from other histories. Her death, the dignity of it, the reverberation of it, its meaning, has escaped us.

There are many kinds of invisibility. Since World War II the tactic of bombing cities has been called strategic bombing. This language makes invisible the fact that civilians are the real targets of these bombs. In a similar way, we make rape in marriage invisible. Because in many states marital rape is still not against the law, it is not measured or counted in our estimates of the number of rapes that take place. And in both cases, law and language only serve to carry out an earlier decision not to see what exists, a decision made by a whole culture, a decision which is itself made invisibly.

It is often said that the child who has been sexually abused wants to return to live with the father who abused her. Many children who are abused, not only sexually but physically and emotionally, are attached to the parent who has abused them. This has even been true for children beaten so badly they have come close to death. By a terrible paradox, the more abused a child has been, the more tenaciously will that child cling to the parent who has abused her. And some children never cease to look in the direction of abuse for love.

We live in a culture which teaches us to look in the direction of abuse for love. We have all been children. For very few of us has the ideal of love and protection which the family promises been realized. And yet we all learned to love in the family. None of us stands outside this system.

None of us stands outside this system, and yet, at the same time, all of us are defined by a larger system, society itself, culture itself, which is both a cause and effect of what goes on inside the family. And when the child who has been raped is returned to her family, so is the question of rape. It is consigned to the domestic world again, to the ghetto of women and children.

When the child is returned to her family she is asked to forgive the father who raped her. And even if she can in this circumstance, at this time in her life, forgive her father, one feels that again a certain burden is shifted away from society and onto the child's shoulders. Forgiveness implies understanding. One needs to understand the causes of such a man's behavior as they exist in the society that shaped him. A man who rapes his own child is possessed of a terrible illness. And it is not an illness of his making alone. It belongs to a whole culture. The tragedy of rape develops from another tragedy, the tragedy through which a man becomes a rapist.

Where is the dividing line between what goes on inside the family and outside the family? They are not really divided. But we have been taught to think of these worlds as separate, as if the truth of one cannot enter the truth of another. It is a dividedness that reflects the dividedness of gender, the world of women and the world of men.

Satyagraha. I take a break from my writing. It is past seven. The sun is down. I walk to the park close to my house. From here you can see the sunset over the bay. The sky is very dramatic, red, gray, blue, huge swirls of cloud looking like fire. Two groups of people stand talking, saying good-bye. And there is a man, alone. Something about him makes me uncomfortable. It is perhaps how uncomfortable he is. He drifts over closer to me, as if without any intention, but the pattern is visible. I am watching the other people and not the sky. When they go, I will go too. I do not want to be here alone with him as it grows dark. On the way back to my house I am acutely aware again that I made the decision to take this walk now because after dark it would be too dangerous for a woman alone. And even though I had been writing about the subject of rape, I made this decision without any thought about what I was doing, imperceptibly.

So many imperceptible decisions, none of them entirely of our own making, shape us into what we call a woman or a man. The influence of culture runs deep into our souls, touching more than the desire to conform. In many ways I depart from convention. I am a lesbian. I live a writer's life. But still there is a certain cast of mind that is mine. One says that women are more sensual, more emotional. But these are not static facts. They are directions, and after one journeys for many years in a certain direction, something has accumulated—we might call it character or knowledge or memory—that makes us who we are.

It is not anywhere in the ordinary habit of a man's thought to enter the mind of a woman who has been or is afraid of being raped. Only recently has the subjective experience of rape entered culture at all. Before now rape was represented in culture mainly by pornography, that is, certainly not from the woman's point of view.

A man hears that his daughter or his lover or his wife has been

raped. His culture has given him a habituated response. He oblit-
erates the experience of the woman who has been raped. He feels
only that his honor has been violated. He has been shamed. And
he may blame her for this. But suppose he has a different response.
Suppose he feels grief and rage for what his daughter has suffered.
Suppose in his imagination he suffers what she has suffered. By
this experience alone he sets himself in a new direction. For him,
what it is to be a man takes on a new dimension.

From every possible quarter we face disaster. The death of the
rain forests. Nuclear war. The accumulation of radioactivity. Acid
rain. The loss of arable land. Famine. These are all events being
born of this culture, of the limitation we place on nature and on
our own nature, partaking of who we are and who we think we
are.

The man who in his mind lets himself imagine the suffering of
a woman moves outside of what is usual for a man to do. And
there are men who are doing this, who are beginning to see what
was before invisible. After his daughter is raped, a man goes for
help to a rape crisis center. He begins to work there. And he finds
he is the only man who does this. And so he forms an organization
for men. And this is one organization among many. There is a
group that teaches young children to defend themselves, to recognize the beginnings of a sexual assault and learn to say no. There
is a group that gives out a telephone number for men to call if
they are feeling violent.

Beyond social action, a certain shift in consciousness is taking
place. The world belonging to men and the world belonging to
women begin to converge at particular points. Masculinity and the
socialization of men are bound up with rape and the history of
rape. Femininity and the socialization of women are also bound
up with rape and its history. And slowly, a new perspective emerges
that allows us to see that no event in society—not government, not

economic life, not warfare—can be understood apart from an understanding of these categories that culture has invented and embellished: the masculine and the feminine.

The masculine values necessary for rape to exist are also the characteristics of the warrior. And women, who have been shaped to submit to masculine values, have allowed war to continue as part of the history of that submission. Perhaps it was with this understanding that Barbara Deming, the great pacifist and feminist writer, wrote, "I have had the dream that women would at last be the ones to truly experiment with nonviolent struggle, discover its full force."

1985. This is a difficult year. Like the huge stockpile of nuclear weapons, signs of disaster accumulate. Last week a friend returned from visiting a small village in Mexico where she overheard a small child speak of nuclear holocaust. "The biggest firecracker," he said.

I read the diary of Etty Hillesum, *An Interrupted Life*. She wrote her pages in the years of the Nazi holocaust, from 1941 until 1943, until she was taken to Auschwitz, where she died. She makes a list of the signs of disaster then. An 18-year-old boy sentenced to death. News of concentration camps. Despotism. Sadism. War. "And yet—" she writes, "at unguarded moments, when left to myself, I suddenly lie against the naked breast of life and her arms around me are so gentle and so protective and my own heartbeat is difficult to describe: so slow and so regular and so soft, almost muffled, but so constant, as if it would never stop."

Just as we are recognizing rape and the sexual abuse of children, just as we turn to face our own shadows, we begin to glimpse a new way of being a woman or a man, a tender space around all that we have bound so tightly with definition.

What we call masculinity and femininity reflect centuries of living within a social system in which men have power over women. One cannot repair the damage of this history simply by combining masculine and feminine characteristics. Rather, we need to explore the genesis of these behaviors and to reach beneath them for what is human, for a response that has not been defined by domination.

Pornography is not written from a woman's point of view. But it is not truly written from a man's point of view either. The man who is portrayed in pornography is there only as a shell. He speaks; he performs. But whatever goes on inside of him—in his mind, in his emotions, or even in his body—is absent. A man's experience of sexual pleasure is not there. Nor is the soul of the man who rapes. When one encounters the images of pornography one does not see in the beginning that these images obliterate both male and female experience.

Images have always had a profound effect on human behavior. A culture both expresses itself and continues itself through imagery. Cultural assumptions, spiritual traditions, even political ideologies are passed on through stories and pictures which appeal to a part of the self that is not always conscious.

A culture that creates rape creates images of rape. These images pass on the ethos of rape, and they encourage rape.* But the path of causation is not always simple. Perhaps a boy sees a pornographic image of a man raping a woman. This images implies that through

---

* In a survey designed by Diana Russell, 930 women were asked, "Have you ever been upset by anyone trying to get you to do what they'd seen in pornographic pictures, movies, or books?" Eighty-nine women, or close to 10%, answered yes. The acts which upset these women included pouring champagne on a woman's vagina, forcing a woman to have coitus with a dog, binding, gagging, beating, and torture. See Diana E. H. Russell, *Sexual Exploitation* (London, 1984). Dr. Edward Donnerstein, University of Wisconsin in Madison, conducted a study in which he found that men who had seen images of sexual violence were more likely to administer what they believed were electric shocks to their partners. Neil Malamuth and James V. Check found the men subjected to films that justify violent sexual behavior tend to believe more readily the myth that women want to be raped. Larry Barron and Murray Straus found in a recent study that the states with the highest rates of rape also had the highest rate of circulation for the most popular pornographic magazines.

rape a man can achieve mastery and pleasure. Years later when he is a man, this image returns to him. We carry all we have ever seen in our memories. For complex reasons, this man has been considering the possibility of becoming a rapist, and the image he remembers affects his decision.

Understanding that pornographic images encourage rape, one part of the feminist movement has supported laws against pornography.* These laws intend to silence pornography. But what does such a silence mean? I suspect this would not be the silence of peace, but rather the silence of denial. The complex reasons that lead a man to rape have not disappeared. The culture that created pornography remains. The culture that shapes the ideas expressed in pornography continues to express itself and to encourage sexual violence in other ways. The way of life that conceives rape still exists.

Pornography is part of a world view. As Adrienne Rich writes, there is no single cause for "the subordination of women, the prevalence of male violence, the emotional asymmetries between men and women, the stunning asymmetries of power." Pornography, rape, and the oppression of women exist together in a kind of field along with racism, poverty, the devastation of the earth, war. Each element in this field acts as both cause and effect. Inside this field, we exist in a kind of perceptual *cul-de-sac*, from which no exit seems possible. That our perception is shaped by this field is part of the politics of consciousness.

Outside this field pornography cannot have the same meaning.

---

*One law has been drafted (in Minneapolis and Indianapolis) that allows a woman who has been raped to sue the publisher or purveyor of pornography in a civil court. Many of those who favor this law have hoped that because the law applies only to civil courts that it will not impede freedom of speech. Yet, though it does not impede this freedom in theory, in practice this law will lead to censorship, and often an invisible censorship. For example, a publisher may decide not to print a book or an article for fear of possible litigation. Moreover, those who can most afford litigation are the pornographers, whereas the publishers of feminist, lesbian, or radical books rarely have the economic means for litigation. For these reasons I believe that in the long run such litigation will do more harm to women than help.

In a culture of equality, a pornographic image cannot cause violence. The man who reads pornography is not innocent of socialization. He has lived his whole life in a society where women are put in subordinate positions. He thinks of himself as one who dominates and does not submit.

In the politics of this consciousness silence is essential. For a man to think of himself as dominant, he must forget that he is dominated by other men and see only that he dominates women. At the same time, the woman who witnesses the symbolic abuse of all women in pornography has probably suffered as a woman in many ways. But the inequities that have caused her suffering are not named. As she submits to this unnamed oppression, she thinks of herself as submissive. It is in this context, a context of silence, in which oppression is invisible, that a man and a woman see a photograph of a man tying up a woman and gagging her.

Pornography uses silence. And it also creates silence. The images of pornography destroy the inner life of both men and women. The experience of a woman, the experience of a man, does not exist in pornography. And above all, the experience of sexuality is erased by pornography.

The pornographer fears sexual experience. Sexuality is, after all, part of the life of the body. Sexual pleasure is not at heart an experience of mastery. It is an experience of loss of control. It is not an experience of dominance but of merging. It is not an experience of power over another but of vulnerability, even vulnerability to one's own feelings. The pornographer tries to master sexual feeling by mastering the female body. But in doing this, he silences sexual knowledge.

The law against pornography does not break out of the context of silence. The legal debate is a debate that goes on in the old field of meaning. What should we be allowed to see? What should we be allowed to know? Such a law can eventually participate in the atmosphere of denial from which pornography derives its power. As if by erasing images of oppression, erasing images of sexual violence, the circumstances that shaped those images would be changed.

When an image is taken from its original context, the meaning of that image is transformed. A feminist can use a pornographic image to reveal another meaning within that image. The same image used to encourage violence in another context yields understanding. Above all, pornographic images give us a hidden truth about our civilization, a truth that civilization tries to deny, a truth that the survivor of rape has encountered. The secret fantasy life of a culture that creates rape is expressed in pornography.

The very fact of oppression, when it is revealed for what it is, works as a force for change. The woman's suffrage movement of the early twentieth century transformed the fact of women's powerlessness in this way. What was before seen as passivity became passive resistance. Women chained themselves to fences or refused to move from the houses of Parliament to support universal suffrage, the right to vote. The image of a woman sitting still, being bound, manacled, and carried off, no longer spoke of degradation and diminishment, nor did it mirror woman's submission to male dominance. Rather, this image challenged domination and the field of circumstances and ideas that supported it.

The perception of women in our civilization is at a fundamental level also the perception of the world. This is part of the truth which rape expresses. That a man is alienated from a woman and does violence to her reflects the essential condition underlying this civilization. The one is alienated from the other. I am alienated from you. One nation is alienated from another. What is human is alienated from nature, from the universe.

When the rapist makes the decision to rape he does not know

he is taking the side of the powerful against the powerless. He has chosen the side of those who have made him submit, who have abused him. He does not see that in rape he violates himself—a self who remembers suffering, a self who perceives injustice, and a self who is, perhaps, capable of love.

Satyagraha. One more decade into the future will it be possible to write that we have experienced a shift in consciousness? Will we have replaced the aridity of rape with another kind of sexuality? Within us lies a sexuality rich and abundant with knowledge. Love which shows us "a thousand slopes in one day and a thousand rivers." Desire. Passion. Pleasure. Ecstasy. This knowledge we have in our bodies for which we hardly have any language, any pictures, any stories. This forbidden knowledge. Satyagraha. What would happen to us if we held this truth?

1985. Seven years have passed. I enter into a dialogue with myself. I ask myself this question: Can there be a world without rape? The atmosphere surrounding a woman's life is still violent. This question cannot be asked apart from many other questions. The violence in a woman's life comes from many sources.

A woman is raped. This happens perhaps not far from where a young soldier stands, guarding the perimeter of a military base. On this base missiles are stationed. They can reach their targets in six minutes. A few miles up the coast a woman pulls her son away from a beach. His legs have broken out in red welts. The ocean here is polluted with waste from a nuclear power plant. A friend tells me she has learned that her mother was raped as a child by her father. And this explains to her some of the unhappiness of her own childhood. Downtown after school adolescents crowd into a movie theater. In the film they watch, the hero is brutal, and he is a womanizer. The women he pursues are stupid and beautiful. A few blocks away a younger child is called a name by a passing stranger. This name refers to the color of her skin. And though she has never heard this name before, she is frightened by the tone of voice. The man in the film is a soldier and he is very strong. The woman who is raped returns to her home without reporting what has happened to the police. Among the children watching the film, in the next few years one will marry, one will give birth out of marriage, and the child will be damaged because while carrying her this mother did not have enough to eat. Another will never find himself, will perhaps join the army, take up odd jobs, wander, find life essentially meaningless. Another will become a lawyer or an engineer or a professor of history. One may be raped. Another may rape.

I read that many trees, not only by the side of the road but deep in forests, evidence a new fragility. It is the air. And the rain, or what is in it. Everything alive begins to seem frail, everything.

1985. The spring of this year was filled with sadness for me. In the winter before, I sat in this room with my friend Elissa. We spoke of our lives, told the stories friends tell each other, what we did, what we said and felt, what we witnessed, what we came to know. Neither of us knew then that she would die. Her death became my grief. It is this we need to understand in this troubled world, we know when we love, our fates are not separate.

PART THREE

Consciousness
1978

I

Solitude. The mind's eye dreaming. The child un-watched. In her room, assuming voices. Afternoon light low through a grove of oak trees: light wind, silence, a small animal in the underbrush. The continuous dialogue. Lakes become sorrow reflected; the sea washes away the inessential. Oneself honed to the core, finally, reaching quiet.

"To destroy the phenomenal world and regain the uncondi-tioned," Mircea Eliade writes of mystical experience, one must "withdraw to the center of oneself." The phenomenal world, in the consciousness of women, in the years since 1971, loomed large; our work was to name conditions which as part of the obscurity of women's actual lives, were before this time, unnamed. We spoke of rape, as we did of abortion, of our economic deprivation, even as we named oppression as a state we knew, prejudice an event from which we suffered. The rhythms of hunger and the needs and crises of children, the dominating requirements of houses, all the bodily needs of families, all the conditions women face daily—this was our traditional work. But in these years, these phenomena widened also, in the minds of women, and we began to see the cares and work of women as social too. Still, these conditions have not changed, and in these years, while I was raising one daughter alone in an economy and society hostile to our needs, I, as many women must, longed for "the unconditioned." But despite our political work, the "unconditioned" was not palpable.

Yet language too is a condition which can determine our behavior as surely as the physical, and language did change. We named. And this naming rent a hole in the way we had been seeing. We *remembered*. And the one I found in my memory was a girl. A girl who loved to be alone in the woods, never worried about grass stains, or wet earth, whose spirit was moved there to see beyond the phenomenal because, when she was alone, she *withdrew to the center of herself*.

And now, eight years after writing of rape and thus naming that actuality to myself, when I return to this subject, the word *solitude* comes to my mouth, and I know I must speak of the fear of rape and what this does to the solitude of women.

All the little girls who were menaced in their solitary journeys— Little Red Riding Hood, Goldilocks—the woods being the place where Snow White could be found if the woodsman had wanted to cut out her heart, and the woods being the place where the bodies of children, most often girls, were found, changed somehow, according to the dark reports, after their abduction. The images. The film that begins in the apartment where a woman had lived alone. Signs of violence. Police standing about. The woman's parents, staring into her dead face, "We begged her not to leave home!" A woman driving alone on the road, stops at a roadside inn, a motel, and in her room, in her shower, is stabbed to death. And is there an echo to the words, "Do not walk here alone at night; do not come to this place unescorted," an echo from a time we cannot remember, but still must sense, as all human history lives in the present in seemingly mysterious signs: the words of the witchburners who said, "When a woman thinks alone, she thinks evil."*

I have been told often not to go into the woods alone. One day I saw a small figure who was watching me on the hill opposite and

---

*Heinrich Kramer and James Sprenger. *Malleus Maleficarum.* trans. Mortague Summers. (Arrow Books, 1971) London, p. 115 (citing Seneca).

across the valley. Could he see that I was a woman? I could see that he was a man. But he turned. Moved up the hill and out of sight. Still halfway across the valley I went into a grove of trees which I felt covered my presence, and waited. Whatever I had come into that valley to work on in my mind was erased now by this struggle. I tried to forget that I had seen him watching me, but I could not. He stayed in my mind even as I called myself foolish to hide, to suppose any danger. Then, as I reached the other side, he appeared suddenly on the path before me. I dropped back, let him walk ahead, waited until, if he had kept on walking, he would be out of sight again. But some sense, a sense that women all have from years of living with this fear, made me go out to the very edge of the path to where I could see around the undulating hill and know for certain he was gone. He was not. He was sitting just behind a curve, just where I would see him only when I was upon him. Now I knew terror. We were half a mile away from the entrance of the park. This was solitude. I grasped some rocks and some sticks and ran by another trail, so that I came out ahead of him on the path. He had started walking, but I was running with a lead and ran the whole distance out of the woods to my car. I waited to confront him, but he must have chosen not to try and overtake me. And so I tried to forget the fear. I went home to work and worked for hours and did forget, forgot so thoroughly, that the incident did not come to my mind, when, at night, I emerged from my study, tired, strangely uneasy in the dark house, and fearsomely lonely. I did not know how I had become such an abandoned creature, cold, and a stranger.

II

Might suffered at the hands of another is as much a tyranny over the soul as extreme hunger . . . when food means life or death. And its empire is as cold, and as hard as though exercised by lifeless matter. The man who finds himself everywhere the most feeble of his fellows is as lonely in the heart of a city, or more lonely, than anyone can be who is lost in the middle of a desert.
—Simone Weil, "The Illiad, Poem of Might"

How does one begin to write about loneliness? One circles the heart of it, describes what is absent. A reassuring presence is not there. Everyone knows loneliness and the battle we meet there. The child must learn that she is separate and that the reassuring presence of her mother can go and can return. Of this genesis of feeling, Lillian Smith writes,

But though we can never quite put the feeling into words, anxiety is not made of mysterious stuff. It is as much of the essence of earthy human experience as is tenderness. Both are feelings that begin to grow during the infant's prolonged helplessness; but are nourished on those inseparable needs of a child to be taken care of and to be related to a human world. Then, it is, when we are so long at the mercy of the Mothering Ones, that we learn our private definitions of tenderness, and loneliness; of sympathy, and terror; in intimacy, and isolation.

And because the need to be taken care of, to survive as a vulnerable creature on the earth, and the need to be related, to love and be loved, are inseparable, in loneliness are encapsulated both the experience of rejection and the fear of death. But how simple the link between rape and loneliness! Aloneness becomes loneliness when one is afraid for one's survival, *endangered*. And of love? But rape, which is a violent attack, must come from hatred. I have always imagined this act as emanating from hatred, a hatred of me, even though the rapist does not know me. Can one's relation to the world be more severely ruptured than by a hatred for oneself by an enemy who does not know one? To be unknown and hated.

And this linkage reaches further. At the same time that she sees there is an "I" who is different from her mother, and from the other, the world, the child begins to perceive herself both as a being and a cause, a force, in the world. She tries to control the comings and goings of her mother. Her life is shaped by the attempt to bring love and caring when she would will them. And finally, as part of this trial, she begins to locate badness in herself. She can be bad, she imagines, she can lose affection because of her badness. *I am left because I am bad*, she says. And isolation is a kind of punishment: the child's room, the prison, solitary. Thus, the rejected reject themselves.

That a grown woman, alone at night, may see herself as rejected, not part of a couple, not chosen, and therefore unworthy, bad in the sense of not good enough, is an evident part of our culture. Yet, when to this rejection is added the intrinsic statement that she is not good enough to be protected (from the violence of rape), and when to this is added a second statement intrinsic to the fact of rape, *someone wishes you harm, someone hates you*, and when to this again is added the old primal fear of death which is part of the threat which always accompanies rape—the weight of loneliness, its invidiousness to the self, can become unbearable.

Yet for the adult consciousness to ever fully experience itself, aloneness must become solitude. This is a hard passage for anyone, coming sometimes unwilled, like a gift, when, as Lillian Smith writes, the chasm between the self and others seems "so narrow that a mere plank would do on which to cross them." Then the world is a sympathetic place which one can enter and leave at will, and so one *wills* to be alone. And it is in this aloneness, Smith tells us, and we know, that one learns. There might be a small anxiety we begin to take with us there on the other side of the chasm, some minor disquiet, which in this quiet of ourselves we can remake, risking newness of perception, perhaps rebuilding or building a different bridge to the world. But the anxiety must be small, and the world a trusted place.

So, to learn aloneness and to begin the learning in aloneness, one must school oneself in trust and will a sympathetic universe into being. But how difficult the existence of rape in that universe makes this willing. Whenever we are alone, in the woods, on a deserted city street, in a house in the country, or an apartment, even in the empty places of some public buildings, we see terrifyingly wide chasms between ourselves and being, because we are in danger.

Solitude. To have this we must give up the sense of being abandoned and learn that the other has freedom of movement. A reassuring presence can leave a room with no cause from us. Our badness does not cause aloneness. We are not bad. Yet what if *someone wants to rape me, someone hates me?*

And of the fear of death itself? Is not one, after all, always alone in the moment of death, and must this not, finally, be accepted if aloneness itself is to be accepted and solitude achieved? Death is change. One loses control. One moves into the unknown. And again, to step into the unknown one must perceive the universe as sympathetic, trust, let go, assume benevolence, that this *is good*, this leap into what could be nothingness. And yet again rape transgresses our solitude. For what if this fear of death comes most often in the fear of being murdered? Murder. Death from malevolence, from hatred, from someone's desire *that I should not exist.*

Not only does someone hate me and want to rape me, but *someone wants me to die.* A knife, a gun, a closed fist, "Stay still, or I will make a jigsaw puzzle of you." The tender of prostitution is money; the tender of rape is violence and death.

We are frightened all of our lives by the incipience of this violence: The rapist may be a stranger, or a man we thought we knew. The act of rape for women is of its very nature never predictable, never *chosen*, never a fight one has wagered on, always a surprise attack, and for no reason. In the moment of rape a woman becomes anonymous. Like all victims of terrorism, there is something awesomely accidental about her fate. She is like the duck flying in formation which the hunter chose to shoot down—she appeared in his gunsight. Absorbed by his violence, her soul and the history of her soul are lost, are irrelevant.

III

And when our parents tucked us into bed and were safely hidden in the living room, we would pop out of bed like jack-in-boxes and dance with the shadows or furtively bring beneath the sheets our toyfriends and fantasies. Some nights it seemed that only the bear staring in the window or the ghost moving in the attic above could get us to be quiet.
—Mary M. Watkins, *Waking Dreams*

Yet for the child, nothing is ever irrelevant or lost, and that part of us which is child-like and still alive, accepts all experience with wonder and does not discriminate. So the intellect may say that rape is merely a casualty, a mistake, and irrelevant to one's soul, as the experience *is*. But the violence and hatred of the act do not feel irrelevant. The child's mind accepts this act as right and looks for a reason. What does the small girl feel when she is first told why she must be home before dark? What does she believe?

The list of admonitions we must give our daughters is long. Do not look into strange men's eyes. If they look into your eyes, look down, look away. Never talk with strange men or boys. Do not go into alleys, into dark unpopulated streets. Be home before dark. Never accept a ride. The world, even a girl's neighborhood, becomes a mined field.

I was not eager to create this field for my daughter. She must have heard hesitancy in every syllable I pronounced. I labored to let her trust the world. And she had just passed through the age of terrible fears of the dark, when her room was the haunt of grizzly bears and other monsters. These are necessary monsters, the analysts say. They are projections of fears, of anger, perhaps anger at the parent, or of the fear of retribution for small transgressions, or retribution for anger itself and rebellion. They come from the child's psychic struggles and float back upon her consciousness as foreign menaces. When she learns her anger will not destroy, that she cannot harm with her secret thoughts of violence, nor will the world harm her because of them, the bears and ghosts become faint and finally vanish. But that is about the age when a mother must tell her daughter that there are real monsters.

And why are these monsters displeased with her? They are displeased because she is turning from a child to a girl, from a girl to a woman. Like the overlooming and majestic atmosphere in Chinese painting, sexuality washes in the background to this threat to a child's or a woman's existence: our own sexual feeling. Can it be coincidental to these circumstances of our culture (because rape is a circumstance of our culture) that until the last decades, sexual feeling in women has been defined, *sui generis*, as bad? When the witch-burning Church Fathers wrote that women's thoughts, when alone, are evil, they meant this evil to be a sexual evil. "All witchcraft," they wrote in the same text, "comes from carnal lust, which in women is insatiable."

And what misogynist sexual morality waits in the studies done over and over to determine how often women provoke rape? Did she have sexual thoughts? A sexual crisis? Did her movements, her clothing, her assertiveness, her submission, her fear, her fearlessness reveal a desire to be raped? Behind these musings are the old prejudices that the sexual feelings of women are like sirens leading men to rash actions against their better selves, as if these feelings have in fact an inherent badness which naturally find their correlative in the world in male brutality. (The child's anger come back to haunt her again.) Does not the guilt of the one who is raped, that shame of the "victim" so often called irrational, or even priggish, does it not in this ancient woman-hating frame become reasonable? The monster is a fantasy. But if the monster becomes real, if the secret sexual life which has for centuries been called sinful is embodied and is menacing, then how eloquent is this affirmation of one's own evil.

These gestures seem so commonplace among women—we draw the window shades before undressing, pull a cloth quickly over the middle of our bodies, cross our arms over our breasts. Thus we imagine we protect men from themselves. The very existence of our bodies then, our own gestures say, is provocation to violence; our bodies become *things* which we must hide. How does one move about the world in this body which has the power to invoke malevolence against oneself?

Are not all our acts judged against this power of our bodies? There is a narrow pantheon of images inside which we are supposed to exist. These images have little to do with the living of our lives nor with the felt moments within us, and yet they ride over our experience and admonish us. They constrict our consideration of our own behavior, invading even our private thoughts, limiting our dreams, and the width that desire might be able to give to our imaginations. This power of our bodies is not the same as the power of being one can experience within oneself; this is a power which exists only in relation to male desire: the power to attract, the power to inspire desire, the power to allow or not allow. Thus the images in this pantheon are sadly limited to what pleases or does not please the male, the one who has power over us. There is the seductress, the *femme fatale*, the Lady of Camellias, the manipulatress who uses male desire. There is the frigid woman who does not use male desire (and ironically, the lesbian is cast into this circle, since her sexuality does not exist in relation to male pleasure). There is the good woman, the wife, the one who knows the true exchange value for her body. And finally there is the child-woman, the pure, whose innocence is a sign of stupidity, who believes she is liked for herself; she was "born yesterday," and the rape or ridicule she receives is a lesson for us all.

But what of our own desire? What of our experience of our bodies as we are inside ourselves, not as provocation but as being? This culture is a *cul-de-sac* for the power of women. Desire itself is seen as provocation. The professors seek to prove in their studies that women are raped because we want rape. Our own desire, which is inseparable from our power in the world, because desire must be the beginning of all action, becomes the harbinger of violence, the feelings in our bodies dangerous to our bodies, we enemies of ourselves, our badness to want, the monsters real.

And if we recover our desire, refuse these admonitions, reject the arguments this culture of rape makes against us, still we live with the fact of rape and the fact that men do see sexuality in women as an invitation to attack. And so this sexual impulse at the heart of our bodies which is the impulse outward and toward the world, a reflection and material of all feeling and thus wedded to our strength as animal creatures must be curbed in the body, even if not in the mind. And our bodies, learning the habit of careful deportment in public places, speak to us steadily and clearly, saying, *you are not free.*

Is it through this illogic and this logic that solitude in a woman's life becomes confinement? The sexual self is by definition solitary. One must be a solitary *being* to desire and move toward union with another. Yet confinement, which so often causes women to be alone, is not solitude. *To destroy the phenomenal world*. Because confinement is phenomenon. It is caused from the outside and is therefore alien to *the center of oneself*, the polar opposite of the unconditioned.

The phenomenon for instance of her children. She must stay home with the children. The confinement of her pregnancy. The confines of her labor. Her house. And the confinements of time in domestic labor (the hour of the infant's rising, the bedtime hour, mealtimes). And the rhythms of her mind defined by the continuous possibility of demand—interruption that is expected—and therefore, unlimited thought unimaginable to her. Her body, always answering to the needs of others, confined by an unnatural tiredness. Her body itself, which might in other circumstances be a touchstone, telling the way to what is real, in the culture of rape, becoming an enemy, and therefore also a confinement. She herself a prison.

"Range is masculine and confinement is feminine," Mary Ellmann writes of the stereotypical ethos. She quotes Freud's letter in which he states of his future wife, Martha Bernays, "I will make every effort to get her out of the competitive role into the quiet, undisturbed activity of my home," as an example of the Victorian sentimentalizing of the confinement of women as shelter.

And this "quiet, undisturbed activity" if it were willed, would sound like solitude perhaps, a kind of meditative space. But Ellmann draws another meaning from it. She invokes the world *practicality* as woman's sphere, a sphere not chosen, but enforced upon her by the same male world of power which has idealized her condition. "This is a forgivable limitation," Ellmann writes sardonically of this confining image, "as long as they shut their mouths and chill the beer. But unfortunately many tend to form and then to express narrow and hostile opinions of masculine projects, and some may even prevent their realization." Thus women, by providing the fire and food which make male creativity possible, because of this very confinement to practicality are depicted as too stupid to recognize male genius—as in the woman employed as a housemaid who was reported to have started a fire with Carlyle's manuscript of *The French Revolution*, or as in Nora Joyce's concern that her husband wasted paper. But Ellmann aims more at the heart of this deprivation when she writes,

Even falling off a cliff, the mother thinks, Mother of Three Falls Off Cliff. And drowning, she cannot review her entire life as she should, her concern being entirely confined to the now forever unshaken unfolded beach towel on the beach.

The tragedy of such images is that we may take them into ourselves; we may become them; certainly our souls suffer from them. And at the essence of this image of woman as narrow and practical is such a severe lack of concern for her being, that indeed, in this view, her soul disappears.

Where can the soul of a woman go in this world? Outside her house is the phenomenon of rape, waiting to confirm her own evil, even to destroy her. And inside? All the phenomena of the needs of others. The value of her life is predicated on her service to others. (And this practical service, contingency, maintenance, what de Beauvoir calls "immanence," always the opposite of the creative—which even when directed toward the "other" is still an expression of self.) Her existence, ringed by an impersonal atmosphere of hatred, is, at its core, of no *intrinsic* value. Does she *have* a soul?

Patriarchy has insisted until the twentieth-century (when the question of souls has been deemed unscientific) that women do not have souls, or if we do, that they are small. This insistence is of itself a phenomenon—*you have no soul, your mind is limited, your world is trivial*—this voice a shaping influence. How well the voice of patriarchy echoes the phenomena which make it seem impossible for women to *regain the unconditioned!*

IV

Every woman's death diminishes me.
        —Adrienne Rich, "From an Old House in America"

To regain the unconditioned. Mrs. Ramsey, a female character created out of the consciousness of female experience and genius (whose character was in fact based on the life of Virginia Woolf's mother, Julia Stephen), does have a soul, and in Woolf's *To the Lighthouse* she reaches through the conditions of traditional female life to touch upon it:

Children never forget. For this reason, it was so important what one said, and what one did, and it was a relief when they went to bed. For now she need not think about anybody. She could be herself, by herself. And that was what now often she felt the need of—to think; well, not even to think. To be silent; to be alone. All the being and the doing, expansive, glittering, vocal, evaporated; and one shrunk, with a sense of solemnity, to being oneself, a wedge-shaped core of darkness, something invisible to others. . . . When life sank down for a moment, the range of experience seemed limitless.

"Not as oneself," finally she realizes in this meditation, "did one find ever, in her experience (she accomplished here something dextrous with her needles) but as a wedge of darkness. Losing personality, one lost the fret, the hurry, the stir . . ."

This observation is part of every religion: to gain serenity one must lose the outward self; to find the soul one must renounce the *ego.* And thus it has often been said of women, that because we deny ourselves, our needs, our egos, we are more spiritual.

Still, real instances of female spirituality are effaced from history, denied, or punished, and this common idea of the spirituality of female nature does not include the religion of those women who were burned at the stake as witches, nor is it really meant to include the voices of Joan of Arc, nor the mystical visions of St. Teresa of Avila, nor of Hildegarde von Bingem, nor the lives of medieval abbesses, nor beginners of the early Marian tradition, nor the female Christian mystics after the dicta of Paul. Because the patriarchal description of female experience does not assume the existence of a self through which to voyage to a communion with what is beyond the self, and women are never, in this spirituality, supposed to speak directly with the universe.

This is the sense in which women are supposed to be more spiritual than men, in the same sense that womanhood itself is by definition a renunciation in favor of men. The Catholic Church canonized Maria Goretti because, though she did not submit willingly to rape, she refrained from attacking her attacker and forgave her murderer, renouncing her rage for charity. Women attend church. We light candles, we make certain, though it is men who read and are illumined by the texts, that religion exists in the home. Even our own spirituality must be renounced for others, because the *raison d'être* of our souls is to save men.

So Dostoyevski's character Sonia Semyonovna discovers and saves Raskolnikov's soul. But her efforts are innocent of original thought (or at times one feels, any consciousness at all). Raskolnikov is the genius. Sonia has no answer to his super-rational questioning. She is nearly mute and can only read him the holy scriptures. Her persuasion is by example, and the example she offers is a selflessness, not born of, but shaped and sharpened by a steadfast and unwavering love for the genius. Her love is truly spiritual, and this in exclusion of bodily sensation. One feels, in the purity of her love for Raskolnikov, her body would get in the way. (And, after all, it is a soiled body.) And yet her example is not particularly to be followed by him. Rather it is the selflessness of her love which finally bears upon him, impresses him. And forgiveness and not passion is her real gift. Forgiveness is at the apex of her healing power. But what does she forgive? She forgives the murder (*Every woman's death diminishes me*) of another woman.

And what is Sonia Semyonovna's experience? In his introduction to the Vintage edition of *Crime and Punishment*, Ernest Simmons writes,

It is a tribute to Dostoyevski's genius that he is able to breathe the breath of real life into a character whose nature is so passive and submissive. Although she reminds one of an allegorical personification of some abstract virtue in a medieval morality play, Sonia transcends her allegorical significance through the sheer force of the novelist's art.

If the shape of this woman's experience is determined by the needs of the errant masculine soul to which she devoted herself, the feel of her experience is so faint that, were it not for masculine genius, one would not know it at all. Her experience scarcely exists.

Her experience is like the experience of Maria Goretti. After her death, the child effected the transformation of the man who raped and murdered her. He saw the light and afterwards devoted his life to serving a holy order of monks. But Maria Goretti, the agent of his miraculous experience, has no experience of her own. Her story is dominated by the story of *his* salvation. She is dead. And Sonia has none, for she does not have enough consciousness, or self, to experience. And yet that is the essence of the spiritual *experience*. And one must have a self, and an awareness of self, in order finally to strip it away, and know a deeper order of being.

How can one learn from the act of giving up what one has never possessed? Such a soul cannot be said to exist.

But Maria Goretti was a girl, not yet grown, and Sonia is a fiction, part of a pantheon of female virtues who are made to appear lifelike through "sheer force." In life, the movement is otherwise. Women are real, full of experience, and possessing soul; force works daily to rob us of self, of consciousness of self and of our souls.

V

In her essay, "The Iliad, Poem of Might," Simone Weil writes, "Might is that which makes a thing of anybody who comes under its sway. When exercised to the full, it makes a thing of man in the most literal sense, for it makes him a corpse."* Yet that is not

---

*For calling my attention to this essay by Simone Weil and its relevancy to these questions regarding rape I am indebted to Michele Cliff for her work in an unpublished paper, and for conversations with her on this subject.

the only sense in which force reduces, not the most common way that force acts, for it is the fear of violence, more than acts of might themselves, which reduces us to less than ourselves, daily. The question of tyranny, for the dead, is over. And for the living, tyranny manifests itself not so much through acts carried out as through acts threatened. In the same essay Weil writes,

The might which kills outright is an elementary and coarse form of might. How much more varied in its device; how much more astonishing in its effects is that other which does not kill; or which delays killing. It must surely kill, or it will perhaps kill, or else it is only suspended above him whom it may at any moment destroy. This of all procedures turns a man to stone.

Or turns a woman to stone. For more than rape itself, the fear of rape permeates our lives. And what does one do, from day to day, with *this* experience, which is, after all, experience which denies experience, experience which says, without words and directly to the heart, *your experience, your existence, may end, at any moment*. Your experience may end, and the best defense against this is not to be, to deny being in the body, as a self; as we teach our daughters, to avert your gaze, make yourself, as a presence in this world, less felt.

How this less felt presence of women reverberates in the politics of sexuality! Politics is in its essence the relation between beings, the I and the thou, the one and the other. The same set of beings who define us as Other is the one who rapes us, or threatens us with rape and violence, and those are the same beings who govern us. Our governors threaten us daily with violence: we live under tyranny.

For the flavor of the fear of rape is not the same, for instance, as that fear the colonialist may feel when he confronts the terrorism of the guerilla. The guerilla is not his governor. He is the one who wields power over the guerilla, and though this terrorist may wish to reduce his governor to a thing, he cannot. Only the confluence of a threat to one's existence and power over how one conducts one's life can cause this unholy transformation.

"From the power to transform him into a thing by killing him there proceeds another power, and much more prodigious, that which makes a thing of him while he still lives," Weil writes. How do we tolerate this? But that toleration is a creation of tyranny. Weil continues,

He is still living, he has a soul, yet he is a thing. A strange being is that thing which has a soul, and strange the state of that soul. Who knows how often during each instant it must torture and destroy itself in order to conform? The soul was not made to dwell in a thing; and when forced to it, there is no part of the soul but suffers violence.

To torture and destroy itself in order to conform—how well, as women, we know those words! How well we know this state of being, where being is not ours. And how much more subtle this second violence. For the first violence is undeniable. One sees the corpse. Who can dismiss the oppression of the maimed or murdered? But fear works a quieter course, less decipherable—like the threat from which violence proceeds, the marks are invisible, yet there and indelible, and choking all movement, for once we move from fear, terror accompanies every outward motion, and we are diminished.

So the position of women is identical to the vanquished, enslaved, and captured, of whom Weil writes in all respects except one. Not only our bodies, but our sexual selves are threatened, ringed with hatred, tyrannized. It is our sexuality which is the focus of the rapist and his wish to possess and humiliate. Sexual humiliation is the core of the act of rape. Eros. Attraction. Impulse toward. Adoration. Passion. These are powerful—the experience of these are powerful. So too must be the humiliation and denigration of these, the force against the willed force of these feelings.

This malevolent answer from the Other to one's sexual being sounds deeply in the body, and the threat of the act of rape is inherent in the dominance of men. How can women love men? Again Weil's words bear on us,

On no occasion has the slave a right to express anything if not that which may please the master. This is why, if in so barren a life, a capacity to love should be born, this love could only be for the master. Every other way is barred to the gift of loving, just as for a horse hitched to a wagon, the reins and bridle bar all directions but one.

Women do love men. But how? In "The Maids," Jean Genet gives to one of the maids the line, "Slaves cannot love," and this in a drama which displays the hatred of the maids toward each other, and hence toward themselves. It is commonplace to say that love must come after self-love. Yet how can women, who have consented to be women, love ourselves? To consent to be a woman is to consent to renunciation of self. There is no one to love. To love or to be loved. The hitched passion must be something else, perhaps the desire to be like the master, or, love of power, or gratitude that she is not finally, murdered. Or perhaps passion will exist in any way possible, even though the stage for its enactment be the same stage on which female passion has been called evil and has met violence. This is the only place her passion is allowed to be.

Does this not illuminate the special sexual violence reserved for the woman who is, or who is perceived to be, a lesbian? Raped. Beaten. Limbs broken. For men who love men, the police, and gangs of young men (looking for the effeminate to punish and brutalize in a man's body), must be feared. Women who love women must fear the violence, or the desired violence, of all men.

Like all real tyranny, there is no escape. A woman who recreates self love, and loves other women, is still living in a world shaped by the act of rape. A woman who loves a man who has chosen not to dominate, to disassociate himself from the power of rape, is still threatened by rape from other men. And yet, because we survive, and the soul emerges and reemerges and will not be quiet, we are proud. We do not, most of us, go about fearfully. This would give to the other even more power. We assert our dignity. We cannot be touched, we say to ourselves. We exist outside desecration and enslavement. So that when the act of rape becomes actual, even if we are not ashamed, even if we do not falsely imagine this act as an emblem of our evil, still some life in us crumbles. We have been made to recognize tyranny and what has been taken from us, made to see by force that we have become powerless. And this knowledge, even while it enrages, destroys.

So, finally, Iphigenia, so that she will not be destroyed chooses her own death, for if it were forced upon her, she would not die as herself.

VI

We who witness Iphigenia's death cannot accept it. The oracle has said to Agamemnon that he must sacrifice his daughter in order to go to war. In Euripedes, the struggle over this decision is played out by a man and a woman, Agamemnon, the girl's father, and Clytemnestra, her mother. The tension of the play is nearly unbearable; it is as if all existence cries out against this death, and yet, we know who will win because we know who has the power. All the action of the play has about it the odor of inevitability, not as a chance happening of blind fate, but as the predictable outcome of a system of dominance, the one over the other, that *is* blind.

So the death of the child must be preceded by a revelation of Clytemnestra's history at the hands of Agamemnon. We must know that she was taken by force into marriage. We must hear Agamemnon, in another discussion, assert that his will is law, and hear Clytemnestra respond, with irony, "I have mastered the art of submission." We must know that the one has power over the other. And, in his unlimited power, we must know of Agamemnon that he did not stop at slaughtering the sacred animals to feed his armies; that he knows the oracle to be false; that his war is waged not so much for justice but for power and the domination of riches.

In these circumstances lie the seed of Iphigenia's death. But this is also the death of Clytemnestra. In pleading for her daughter's life she cries, "Don't make an evil woman of me," for this death, and her recognition of her powerlessness to prevent it, must seal her to hatred.

But Agamemnon does not escape fate dictated by might either.

He, too, is turned to stone. Iphigenia, in asking for her own life, says to her father that she wishes she had the voice of Orpheus that she might be able to charm even the stones and thus win his love. It is his love that would allow her to live. She is dependent on that. But he has turned to stone. Had she the voice of Orpheus, a male voice, she might charm even stone. But she is female; her voice has no such power. Her state is the same as her mother's. "If you kill me, you also kill her," she says and these words, together with Clytemnestra's plea, "Don't make an evil woman of me," reverberate through the play. Iphigenia dies a physical death and thus becomes a thing; Clytemnestra is reduced to an object while she lives, in Weil's words, "a life that death has frozen long before extinguishing it." Because, as Weil writes, "That a human being should be a thing is from the point of view of logic, a contradiction; but when the impossible has become a reality, that contradiction is as a rent in the soul."

As a rent in the soul. Such is the power of the phenomenal world on the lives of women, and this is how cunning the *cul-de-sac* of our situation is, that when we would shed this phenomenal world, and draw deep to the center of ourselves so that we might regain the unconditioned, when we seek solitude, we are most in danger from this phenomenal world. And is this not a religious problem? Before every epiphany, and before each revelation or initiation into the sacred, one must admit ignorance. One must be blank. Give up assumptions, and shed ego, the daily self. Be prepared to leap into emptiness.

Emptiness. The dark. The abyss. The edge of death. Union and loss of self. Falling. The unknown depths. The void. The moment of transformation is a leap of faith. One trusts existence. Emptiness and the unknown, even in shapelessness, become benevolent. As Weil writes "something stronger than I was compelled me for the first time in my life to go down on my knees." But that something stronger must be felt as good, that which one wants to be part of, as the light, as the universe, not that which would reduce one to a thing.

Yet for women, the dark, deserted space, unknown geography is not safe. For us, *emptiness implies a malevolent presence*. And is it by accident that in the same mythos in which Iphigenia is sacrificed to her father's religion so that he might wage war, Zeus establishes his power first by raping his mother and then by raping his wife? Or that the king of gods has chained Hera by golden bracelets and anklets to chasten her for challenging his power? This same Zeus, as the father of Persephone, gave Hades his blessing for the abduction of his daughter into hell, while Demeter, her mother, suffers this rape as her own, this loss as a part of herself gone.

But one cannot say that the human father, Agamemnon, does not suffer his daughter's death. The play is a play about his choice; we watch the play of this decision on his psyche. "Such is the nature of might. Its power to transform a man into a thing is double and it cuts both ways; it petrifies differently but equally the souls of those who suffer it and of those who wield it." When one is the malevolent presence, emptiness becomes more than frightening; this void is hell. And in the act of experiencing might, to reduce another to a thing, the rapist suffers the consequences of the universe he has created and which he must then inhabit. This universe is ruled by might, and he himself is subject to it. The tyranny of might does not destroy his self, but rather constructs a self that is inimical to revelation. Revelation, after all, comes only through vulnerability, both in men and in women. The armored warrior cannot see. One must admit *one does not know*, one must give up control. If the imagined spirituality of women is false because it has derived from an absence of being rather than being, the spirituality of men is totally subjugated to the self of the phenomenal world. And hence has religion in patriarchy gotten a reputation for hypocrisy; the missionary precedes the imperialist; the holy fathers are greedy; religion is something which must be unmasked, because all it is is a mask. And like might, those on both sides of a mask suffer.

The religion of the fathers is part of the phenomenal world which one must destroy before regaining the unconditioned. And in the unconditioned, when the paradigms of patriarchy have been cast away, exist new vision, new possibility.

Once this phenomenal world is repudiated as the only real world, conditions which patriarchy has pronounced as natural or inevitable fall into a different light. All that which has been posed to us as scientific and objective truth, in this state, where we are withdrawn to the center of ourselves, can be questioned. In this light, the very way patriarchy sees loses force. The act of rape which embodes a denial of the existence of the other as a real being with a soul, has its analogue in a patriarchal consciousness, a view of the universe, which denies intelligence in that which is perceived. As Mary Daly writes in *Beyond God the Father*, "Widening of experience so pathologically reduced can come through encounter with another subject, an I who refuses to be an It."

To refuse to be an It. In this there is joy, whatever the phenomenal outcome.

But must phenomenon and spirit always be split, as if one were the enemy of the other? Do they not in the end always rejoin? At the end of the nineteenth century, Susan B. Anthony, the political leader, pleaded to Annie Besant, the spiritual leader,

Annie—why don't you make that aura of yours do its gallivanting in this world, looking up the needs of the oppressed, and investigating the causes of present wrongs? Then you could reveal to us workers just what we should do to put things right, and we could be about it.

Annie Besant "sighed and said that life was short and aeons were long, and that while everyone would be perfected some time, it was useless to deal with individuals here." To which Susan B. Anthony exclaimed, "But Annie! We *are* here!"

We are here now, and we see, and there are things that we know. In the same motion with which we have denied the naturalness of the phenomena imposed upon us, we have discovered ourselves. Of this Mary Daly writes,

In the rising consciousness of women, power is experienced as the power of presence to ourselves and each other, as we affirm our own being against and beyond the alienated identity bestowed upon us within patriarchy.

And against and beyond this alienation, within our very beings whose presence is now powerful to us, we have found knowledge. This knowledge of how the phenomenal world might be must have been hidden within us for ages, for this is familiar and simple, and has that quality of certainty which separates vision from desire or belief. We *know* that a world without rape is possible. This world exists in our minds, exists even in some of our lives.

We know this as we know the feel of air in our lungs, irrefutably. And along with this, we know other things which make up the dimensions of this world. In this world, the lives of other beings are held as sacred, as is the life of the self. The body of woman is cherished. Desire in that body is loved, and the spirit in that body is visible and recognized in the smallest daily movements. This world is real to us because we have felt it in our bodies, and because of its beauty and healing presence, even the questions we have about the nature of this world take on for us as much reality as the phenomena which still confine.

Would not, we ask, the recognition of sacredness in the other, of the spirit in the other, and this cherishing of a woman's body need to spring from a whole weave that must also include a different notion of power; one that acknowledges the power in each being, but eschews power over another being as a lower order of behavior? Would not this weave have to include the erasing of the possibility of other kinds of cruelties for which rape might be a metaphor? Could theft of food from the mouths of children exist in this world, or any murder of body or soul? What kind of mind finds rape unimaginable?

What does the inside of my mouth feel like when even the memory of rape has vanished. And how is it then, walking into the night, the first steps into the sweet, safe, covering darkness? And where do these steps take us? Are there mysteries outside our windows which will be revealed to us when we know the air is safe there? Who are we when we are finally safe with our own kind? Our kind. And what of the silence when there is no more such cruelty even imaginable as rape, what is the softness like inside such a silence, such a solitude. I have a taste of it now; it brings me near tears. I know this world we see the edges of is real. And because we see this world, we can make it be.

And as I write these words, I can almost see the night outside my window transform. But I know too, setting these words here how real are the forces against us, those who cannot or will not imagine things differently. Those who in some contortion of their minds believe they need rape, and all that goes with rape, to exist in this world. But I know too the world has changed before and the seemingly unchangeable has become different. And if I am asked to be cynical because of facts and numbers and probabilities, or defeats or imperfections in our efforts to change, or because of weapons which can destroy the earth or time and space which grow too precious, I answer that what I feel, even in the face of all this, is a joy in the possibility I see. To think of that night as a safe and covering place! So if I choose hope over dread, it is not only that I prefer hope in my bones, which I do, but that I have tasted freedom from fear, a world we imagine, and this small taste means more to me than large fears. This then, is not so much a conviction of the inevitability of the outcome, but a powerful feeling of being which is the knowledge that sustains me. We are, as Susan B. Anthony said, on this earth. *We are here.* This is *our* place, the place of our imaginings, the place of our lives.

We are here. In *this* world, while the act of rape reverberates around us, destroying the unconditioned, emptiness, the possible. But if the act of rape has had the power to sever the phenomenal from the unconditioned, to reduce souls to things, keep us from the centers of ourselves, from self, or make of religion a mask, we know another power, and because we exist, we can know this well; a power not a might, not exerted over another, and a knowledge not separated from ourselves or others. We know. We have the power of being no force can resist. *We are here.*

PART FOUR

The Power of Consciousness: *A Collage*

compiled by Sandy Boucher and Susan Griffin

In this collage, we have woven together words from the feminist movement, events from our recent history, and reflections from the patriarchy, both ancient and modern, about women, all bearing on the subject of rape and the power of consciousness to change our lives. This collection is necessarily partial and its weavings eccentric, but we trust it to ring back into the life of each reader, so that her own experience resonates with the stories, the statements made, the wisdom revealed in these documents. We ring the bell; the response is hers.

> *Sandy Boucher and Susan Griffin*
> *Berkeley, California, Winter Solstice, 1986*

In order that we stop being victims, we ourselves must take up the struggle against rape. Individually and collectively we can break the silence and make it no longer a taboo subject, or something shameful which weighs us down.

> French witness. In Diana E. H. Russell and Nicole Van de Ven (Eds.), *The Proceedings of the International Tribunal on Crimes Against Women*, 1976

Few Latinas could fail to believe Inez Garcia's inability to describe the experience of rape to the policemen who arrested her.

We are painfully shy about our bodies and about sex. When she later complained of pains "down there" to a woman prison attendant, she was taken to a doctor who reportedly implied that Inez was upset, imagining things, and didn't examine her. . . .

We Latinas are not encouraged to be articulate about any part of our experience, much less about sexual abuse. . . .

In the courtroom she decided to defy the twin *macho* assumptions of Latin culture, that a woman belongs to a man; and that a woman dishonored by belonging to more than one man is herself at fault, as sinful as Eve. She defied the shameful silence with which women, especially Latinas, are supposed to treat their own sexual enslavement. I am grateful to her.

Maria del Drago, *Ms.*, May 1975

"You could have screamed—why did you suddenly lose your voice?"

His words sank deep and bitter within me. For, dominated by a feeling of shame, I believed them. I could not face him, could not be entirely honest and open about such things—it was too shocking, too shameful; I was not entirely conscious of their truth. I was too poisoned with shame and dishonesty about sex to face any situation clearly.

Agnes Smedley, *Daughter of Earth*, 1973

When the defiled female says, "That is the gentleman who raped me," we need corroboration. If her jaw is broken, for example, that is proof of force. Otherwise, how do we know she was raped? The difference between rape and romance is a very thin line.

N.Y. State Assemblyman Joseph F. Lisa, *Redbook*, September 1972

In Holland rape is a hidden problem. The police admit that rape exists, but when a woman comes to them to report a rape, the reaction is often that she has provoked it. Very often she is not treated seriously. That's why the group "Vrouwen tegen verkrachting" (Women against rape) started in Amsterdam in November

'75. . . . In the first month we opened our center, we got 150 phone calls from women who had been raped or assaulted.

> Dutch witness. In Diana E. H. Russell and Nicole Van de Ven (Eds.), *The Proceedings of the International Tribunal on Crimes Against Women*, 1976

Mamie Carter said firmly, "If you look at the laws covering rape you'll see they all stem from the property code. Now Almeta—at sixty-five a woman is not considered of much value as property so her rapist wasn't even indicted. And if she is black too she's not even believed. The fact is, people feel sex is obscene with the old, but you all read the tittering between the lines. The fourteen-year-old girl was property not really damaged since her hymen was left intact, so her rapist was allowed to plead to a lesser sentence.

> June Arnold, *Sister Gin*, 1975

So determined were the Levites that a reverent regard for the paternity of children be developed that among them even violent rape was equated with marriage, much as it was among the Indo-European-controlled Assyrians. In Levite law, the rape of a virgin was honored as a declaration of ownership and brought about a forced marriage.

> Merlin Stone, *When God Was a Woman*, 1976

If a damsel that is a virgin be betrothed unto an husband, and a man find her in the city, and lie with her;

Then ye shall bring them both out unto the gate of that city, and ye shall stone them with stones that they die; the damsel, because she cried not, being in the city; and the man, because he hath humbled his neighbour's wife: so thou shalt put away evil from among you.

But if a man find a betrothed damsel in the field, and the man force her, and lie with her: then the man only that lay with her shall die:

But unto the damsel thou shalt do nothing; there is in the damsel no sin worthy of death: for as when a man riseth against his neighbour, and slayeth him, even so is this matter:

For he found her in the field, and the betrothed damsel cried, and there was none to save her.

If a man find a damsel that is a virgin, which is not betrothed, and lay hold on her, and lie with her, and they be found;

Then the man that lay with her shall give unto the damsel's father fifty shekels of silver, and she shall be his wife; because he hath humbled her, he may not put her away all his days.

Deuteronomy 22:23–29

The interviewer: Do you see rape as much worse than physical assault, or do you see it as equivalent?

Ms. Gold: I see rape as being worse in that it doesn't come from a need for money and it doesn't come from total insanity either. Whatever it is that causes someone to hit someone else is horrifying in a different kind of way. Rape seems to be so imbedded in our society. It seems just a natural outcome of the way that men are. And that is a really frightening thing.

Diana E. H. Russell, *The Politics of Rape: The Victim's Perspective,* 1975

Allowing a male friend into your home who turns violent and rapes you cannot be prosecuted in court. In the eyes of the court, allowing the male into your home implies consent for him to have sexual intercourse with you. The courts apparently see that opening your front door to a man means that the vagina is opened to his penis. As brash and boorish as these conclusions may sound, we must understand that they constitute the thinking of society and the courts, not of women.

Kathy Barry, in *Stop Rape* (pamphlet), 1972

People in Scandinavia have a reputation for being free and tolerant. According to criminologists, Scandinavian police are considered the least corrupt in the Western world. Nevertheless, if a woman has trespassed just a few steps outside the limited sphere of her accepted premises, she will be met by suspicion if she accuses anyone of raping her, or she will be downright disbelieved. If Scandinavian women really behaved as the liberated women people in many countries think we are, we could not count on being respected and treated with dignity.

In Diana E. H. Russell and Nicole Van de Ven (Eds.), *The Proceedings of the International Tribunal on Crimes Against Women*, 1976

Rape is a punishment without crime or guilt—at least not subjective guilt. It is punishment, rather, for the *objective* crime of femaleness. That is why it is indiscriminate. It is primarily a lesson for the whole class of women—a strange lesson, in that it does not teach a form of behavior which will save women from it. *Rape teaches instead the objective, innate, and unchanging subordination of women relative to men.*

Barbara Mherof and Pamela Kearon, *Notes from the Third Year: Women's Liberation*, 1972

There is not real affliction unless the event which has gripped and uprooted a life attacks it, directly or indirectly, in all its parts, social, psychological, and physical. . . . Affliction causes God to be absent for a time, more absent than a dead man, more absent than light in the utter darkness of a cell. A kind of horror submerges the whole soul. During this absence there is nothing to love. . . . That is why those who plunge men into affliction before they are prepared to receive it are killers of souls.

Simone Weil, *The Simone Weil Reader*, 1977

The souls of women are so small
That some believe they've none at all.

Samuel Butler, *Selections from Notebooks*, 1950

I was raped by my father's best friend when I was 14. My father had died only a little time before this. This situation was really traumatic for me, not solely because of the rape, but mainly because it was the outcome of the rejection I felt by my parents and the lack of love which existed in our family. Afterwards, I was made to feel dreadfully guilty. This man blamed me. The next morning he told me I was a bitch, a whore, a little slut, etc., etc. And when I tried to talk about it, when I tried to say what had happened to me, people threw the same accusations at me. . . . Since I felt so completely put down at that time, I felt I had no choice but physical death or internal death. For years I suffered terribly because of this experience. I was 18 before I managed to speak about it again.

> French witness. In Diana E. H. Russell and Nicole Van de Ven (Eds.), *The Proceedings of the International Tribunal on Crimes Against Women*, 1976

The atmosphere outside the [sorority] houses is less protected. "Hey, horny, over here," some fraternity boys yell at us as we walk across the street. At another house, there is a commotion on the roof. Four frat boys are checking us out and flashing numbers on cardboard from one to ten, judging our comparative assets. All the rushees make a supreme effort not to notice. . . .

It isn't over, not yet—there is still the so-called "pig run."

We girls traditionally pick up our bids—invitations to join a house—and then go running and squealing down frat row to our new homes—at least that's the chauvinistic fraternity version. Hundreds of frat men line the sidewalks on Saturday morning guzzling beer and hooting. . . . Last year, [a young man] tells me, one frat rented a 600-pound hog and brought it to pig run on a leash. It had a sign written on its back that said, "Where's my bid?"

> Amy Linn, San Francisco *Chronicle*, October 2, 1978

I grabbed her from behind, and turned her around and pushed her against the wall. I'm six foot four . . . I weighed about two hundred and forty pounds at this time, and she didn't have much chance to get away from me. She tried. I pulled her back and hit her several times in the face quite hard, and she stopped resisting and she said, "All right, just don't hurt me." And I think when she said that . . . all of a sudden a thought came into my head: My God, this is a human being. . . .

It was difficult for me at that time to even admit that when I was talking to a woman, I was dealing with a human being, because, if you read men's magazines, you hear about your stereo, your car, your chick. . . .

Man who attempted rape at age 17, *Ms.*, December 1972

The childhood of women must be free and untrammeled. The girl must be allowed to romp and play, climb, skate and swim; her clothing must be more like that of the boy—strong, loose-fitting garments, thick boots, etc., that she may be out at all times and enter freely into all kinds of sports. Teach her to go alone, by night and day, if need be, on the lonely highway, or through the busy streets of the crowded metropolis. The manner in which all courage and self-reliance is educated *out* of the girl, her path portrayed with many dangers and difficulties that never exist, is melancholy indeed. Better, far, suffer occasional insults or die outright, than live the life of a *coward*, or never move without a protector. The best protector any woman can have . . . is *courage*.

Elizabeth Cady Stanton. In Gerda Lerner, *The Female Experience: An American Documentary*, 1977

If you wear a bikini or tiny miniskirt to the market, be warned: You are a neon sign asking for trouble.

Today's teen-age girls, with their freedom of dress, youthful trust, and heightened awareness of femininity are particularly choice targets for the sex criminal.

Marla Zellerbach, San Francisco *Chronicle*, June 8, 1970

To be gazed at is one danger; to be manhandled is another. Women as a rule are unfamiliar with violence, they have not been through the tussles of childhood and youth as have men; and now the girl is laid hold of, swept away in a bodily struggle in which the man is the stronger. She is no longer free to dream, to delay, to maneuver: she is in his power, at his disposal. . . . It is not uncommon for the young girl's first experience to be a real rape and for the man to act in an odiously brutal manner; in the country and wherever manners are rough, it often happens that—half consenting, half revolted—the young peasant girl loses her virginity in some ditch, in shame and fear.

Simone de Beauvoir, *The Second Sex*, 1957

I was trained to be numb, I was born to be numbered and pegged,
I was bred and conditioned to passivity, like a milk cow.
Waking is the sharpest pain I have ever known.
Every barrier that goes down takes part of my flesh,
Leaving me bloody. How can I live wide open?

Marge Piercy, "What Is Most Hoped for and Most Feared in the Matter: Judgement," *To Be of Use*, 1973

The sexual abuse of children, who are overwhelmingly female, by sexual offenders, who are overwhelmingly male adults, is part and parcel of the male dominated society which overtly and covertly subjugates women.

Florence Rush. In Noreen Connell and Cassandra Wilson (Eds.), *Rape: The First Sourcebook for Women*, 1974

Lowering her head, she begins walking slowly along under the cliffs. "He's not going to drive me away!" she decides, and shoves her fists deep into the pockets of her jacket. But already the knowledge of his presence has slid like a screen between her and her surroundings. Thoughts rise in her like garbage from the bottom of a pond—sights she would rather forget, stories told by women in the coffee room at work, by her other friends. And she thinks of children. At what young age will a girl child hear that husky, whispered "Hey . . . look!" and turn to see the man in the darkened doorway, the man back among the trees, the man in the window.

Sandy Boucher, "Charm School," *True to Life Adventure Stories*, 1978

With regard to rape in marriage, the law in Portugal states that marital relations have to be maintained. The expression, "He used

me," is the usual way rape in marriage is expressed in Portugal. . . .
The husband seems to be able to use his wife's body in any way
he wishes—to force her to have an abortion she does not want, to
have her sterilized, to lock her up, or to beat her.

> Portuguese witness. In Diana E. H. Russell and Nicole Van de Ven
> (Eds.), *The Proceedings of the International Tribunal on Crimes
> Against Women*, 1976

Woman's body *is* the woman.

> Ambrose Bierce, *Collected Works 1910–1912*

We say our personal problems are political and should have political solutions. In consciousness-raising meetings, we go around
in a circle speaking in turn. This is very helpful in giving each
member a chance to compose herself and her thoughts. . . . The
more concrete, specific, and personal the group can be, the more
information it will have to work with. This body of experience will
lead to your own feminist politics.

> Noreen Connell and Cassandra Wilson (Eds.), *Rape: The First
> Sourcebook for Women*, 1974

I have gone through both these debilitating experiences, these
attacks on my personhood, which rape really is, and yet I am standing here, and I am able to talk to you about this.

> Danish witness. In Diana E. H. Russell and Nicole Van de Ven
> (Eds.), *Proceedings of the International Tribunal on Crimes Against
> Women*, 1976

I am a woman come to speak for you.
I am a woman speaking for us all
From the tongue of dust and fire
From the bowl of bitter smoke.
This is a song for strength and power.

> Meridel LeSueur, "Hush, My Little Grandmother," *Rites of Ancient
> Ripening*, 1975

There was a time when you were not a slave, remember that. You walked alone, full of laughter, you bathed barebellied. You say you have lost all recollection of it, remember . . . you say there are no words to describe it, you say it does not exist. But remember. Make an effort to remember. Or, failing that, invent.

Monique Wittig, *Les Guerilleres*, 1971

"I'd kill a rapist if he tried to force me to submit to his advances," declares Erin Sullivan, a member of NOW.

Erin is not alone in her sentiment.

Recently, members of a group called Women for a Free Future addressed the Berkeley City Council on the subject of rape.

Erin dramatized the session by coming in at the end dressed in black and carrying an unloaded Winchester rifle. She had checked to see if it was legal to carry an unconcealed, unloaded rifle, and it was.

The women from Berkeley feel that they are representative of women all over the world who refuse to put up with rape any more. Among their demands from the Berkeley City Council were that free public transportation be given all women from dusk to dawn, that more streetlights be added . . . that self-defense be taught to female children in the school system and that women be allowed to carry loaded concealed weapons.

Meanwhile a check has disclosed that karate and judo classes in almost every major city are jammed. "I feel a lot safer now that I know karate," one student says. Other karate learners say that their rages go so deep that actually—at times—they fantasize about killing a rapist.

Susan Berman, San Francisco *Examiner/Chronicle*, January 17, 1971

Entrance into radical feminist consciousness implies an awareness that the women's revolution is the "final cause" (pun intended), in the radical sense that it is the cause which can move the other causes. It is the catalyst which can bring about real change, since it is the rising up of the universally and primordially objectified "Other," discrediting the myths which legitimate rapism.

Mary Daly, *Quest*, Spring 1975

Rape Speak-out in New York City, 1971

New York Radical Feminists, Rape Conference, New York City, April 17, 1971

Women Organized Against Rape (24-hour crisis center), Philadelphia, 1971

Women in three blocks of Venice's North Beach organized early in September to combat rape in their neighborhood. Women exchanged personal experiences with harrassment and shared effective methods of self-protection. Women from Los Angeles Rape Crisis Hotline demonstrated self-defense techniques, and suggested such necessary safety measures as dead-bolt locks. A phone tree was organized so neighborhood women would be able to contact each other. The women planned a second meeting to learn more self-defense techniques and to organize other Venice neighborhoods.

Sister, October/November 1977

As part of their prevention efforts, some rape squads have adopted near-vigilante tactics. In East Lansing, Mich., members of the rape crisis center are said to have scrawled "rapist" on a suspect's car, spray-painted the word in red across a front porch, and made late-night warning telephone calls. In Los Angeles, the squad has adopted a counterharassing strategy: When a woman called to complain that a neighbor followed her whenever she went out, squad members followed the follower for three days. That was enough to make him change his ways.

Time, April 23, 1973

Dessie Woods has been in prison for more than two years now. On February 2, 1976, she was sentenced to a total of 22 years in one of the South's most notorious women's prisons in Hardwick, Georgia.

Since that time she has been the victim of brutal beatings, forced druggings, and nude solitary confinement. Her crime?

Dessie Woods dared to successfully fight back against one of the South's oldest traditions: White rape of black women! Her assailant, a white insurance salesman named Ronnie Horne, was killed with his own unlicensed gun, and, as it happens in so many cases, the victim, Dessie Woods, was made to be the criminal, and the dead would-be rapist was made to be the victim.

San Francisco Women's Center Newsletter, July 1978

New Smyrna Beach, Fla.: Two coeds were raped by a man armed with an ice pick but then turned on their assailant and strangled him to death with a scarf after he threatened to kill them. . . .

After reportedly subduing their attacker, the coeds went to a nearby farmhouse and called police. Police said the rape victims believed they had only rendered their attacker unconscious.

San Francisco *Examiner/Chronicle,* June 9, 1974

Thus when a white man rapes a black woman [JoAnne Little], the underlying meaning of this crime remains inaccessible if one is blind to the historical dimensions of the act. One must consider, for example, that a little more than a hundred years ago, there were few black women who did not have to endure humiliating and violent sexual attacks as an integral feature of their daily lives. Rape was the rule; immunity from rape the exception. . . .

There can be little speculation about the turn events would have taken had JoAnne Little been killed by Alligood. A verdict of "justifiable homicide" would have probably closed the books on such a case.

But she had the courage to fend off her assailant. The price of her resistance was a new threat of death, this time issuing from the government of North Carolina.

Angela Davis, *Ms.*, June 1975

San Francisco (UPI): The State Supreme Court Wednesday publicly censured S.F. Superior Court Judge Bernard B. Glickfeld for referring to a rape victim "in an insulting and inexcusable manner."

It was only the second time such judicial discipline has been used by the court. The other case involved Santa Clara County Superior Court Judge Gerald Chargin who was censured for racial remarks about Mexican-Americans.

Daily Californian (Berkeley), January 21, 1971

"We don't want a dyke in our commons," three men reportedly told a woman student at Ohio State University. "If you don't (move out), we'll show you what men are like."

A week later, according to the *YIPster Times*, they demonstrated their maleness to her by beating and raping her, successfully eluding an all-woman defense squad organized to protect her as soon as she had been threatened.

Rape has since become a major issue at OSU, with a "Demonstration of Outrage" by the local Women Against Rape, with a refusal by University Officials to take action other than expressing "concern for the safety" of all students, and with campus police saying they could do nothing because the victim feared retaliation and harassment.

Ammi Bar On of WAR described the shrubs, barriers, and high brick walls of the OSU North dormitory complex as a danger to women. She is helping to recruit and train women marshals for the campus. WAR is also calling attention to the antigay and misogynist attitudes of some male students and hangers-on around the campus. Students were asked to report harassment or gossip about any woman's sexuality to forestall any future attack.

Majority Report, December 10–21, 1977

In 1974 the Ohio legislature passed a law allowing damage suits by victims against rapists. The law has just been tested in a Cleveland court, and a woman was awarded $22,000.

Majority Report, October 15–28, 1977

Although societal attitudes no doubt are responsible for the present construction of rape laws, it is also true that this construction serves to reinforce those attitudes. If the laws were changed to relate more rationally to the reality of the crime and to the goal of sexual equality, attitudes about the crime might also change.

Camille E. LeGrand, *California Law Review*, 1973, 61

Workshop on Rape, sponsored by San Jose NOW, April 29, 1973, issued "Recommendations for Revision of Rape Laws."

Women's Litigation Unit of San Francisco Neighborhood Legal Assistance Foundation, June 22, 1973, issued "Proposed Amendments of the Rape Laws."

In order to place the phenomenon of rape in its legal context, it is also necessary to understand the conceptual framework in which rape laws exist. Here the focal question is "Who or what do rape laws protect?" Legal writers analyzing rape laws have concluded that rape laws protect male interests: Rape laws bolster, and in turn are bolstered by, "a masculine pride in the exclusive possession of a sexual object"; they focus a male's aggression, based on fear of losing his sexual partner, against rapists rather than against innocent competitors; rape laws help protect the male from any "decrease in the 'value' of his sexual 'possession,' " which results from forcible violation. However accurate these conclusions are, it is interesting that these analyses have not focused on a woman's physical integrity, peace of mind, or freedom of movement without fear of sexual attack as fundamental values to be protected by rape laws.

Camille E. LeGrand, *California Law Review*, 1973, 61

Women's Rights Brainstorming Group of American Civil Liberties Union of Northern California, All-Day Rape Meeting, July 17, 1973.

Sacramento: SB 1678, introduced by Senator Alan Robbins, D-Van Nuys, would limit substantially the instances when a rape victim could be questioned about her previous sexual relationships.
Berkeley Gazette, June 13, 1974

[Yvonne] Wanrow, a resident of Colville, Washington, was convicted of second-degree murder last year and sentenced to serve two 20-year prison terms for the admitted 1972 shooting of a convicted rapist, William Wesler. Wanrow claimed the man had threatened both her and her three children.

In an unprecedented move last year, the Washington Supreme Court, however, set aside Wanrow's first conviction and ordered a new trial for the Native American woman. The court stated that "In our society women suffer from a conspicuous lack of access to, training in, and the means of developing those skills necessary to effectively repel a male attack without resorting to the use of deadly weapons." Wanrow had argued that she used a gun on Wesler because she was in a cast at the time, and could not defend herself.
Plexus, July 1977

When Liz Bunding, a white belt in karate, yelled "Eeeeeeccccccccchhhhh!" yesterday afternoon, you could tell she meant it.

It was the women's liberation protest outside the second meeting of a male-only karate class in Harmon Gymnasium at the University of California at Berkeley.

And the ladies, 75 of them, were protesting the ban on females in the class with a karate demonstration of their own. . . . "Women need karate as a means of self-defense," announced a pretty brunette, who refused to reveal her name or age. "They must develop

their bodies physically to gain self-confidence and to lessen their psychological dependence on men."
San Francisco *Chronicle*, January 14, 1970

Lt. Robert B. Johnson of the Berkeley Police Department will speak on "Defensive Tactics for Ladies" for members of the University of California Mothers Club on Tuesday.
Berkeley Gazette, February 25, 1971

Martial arts and self defense study offer a way of self reflection and change. As our concentration grows in our study, the focus involved is a clear meditative concentration permeating the wrenching pushing exertion of our bodies. We have here a way of experiencing the oneness of our mind/body/soul, healing in ourselves the fragmentations and divisions of patriarchy. The style I study is called Ja Shin Do, which in one translation means Art of the New Self.
Emily Erwin Culpepper, *Womanspirit*, Summer 1976

Women employees at the Long Island Jewish Medical Center are being taught forms of karate and ju-jitsu, since they are concerned about their personal safety when they have to walk to their cars in the parking lot at midnight and then drive through deserted streets to their homes.
Female Liberation Newsletter (Boston), August 2, 1971

After the workout/class, we spent the rest of our time talking about the meaning in our lives of martial art study. I shared information about some of the physiological aspects, that is—this kind of overall body workout often produces a calm, exhilarating feeling of well-being, which in part may be due to the stimulation of the right brain, which is so underused and undervalued in our patriarchal, linear, technical-mind culture. Also, for many women, our determination to study a martial art is often the first time we have really taken physical development and strength potential of our bodies seriously. For women with previous athletic backgrounds, martial art study often has a new sense of woman-identified purpose. I find that I learned the lessons of patriarchy in my muscles and sinews, as well as in my mind and soul; and this martial art study is both an UNconditioning process, as well as the conditioning and creating of a new self.

Emily Erwin Culpepper, *Womanspirit*, Summer 1976

In Milan recently, 400 girls stormed a local high school. They punched teachers and staff, broke into a classroom and dragged out Sergio Brambilla, an 18-year-old student.

They shoved him into the school cafeteria, where they conducted their own trial. The girls accused Brambilla of raping his girlfriend in a car and then threatening her with a gun not to report him. The girls found him guilty and beat him severely.

Parade, June 26, 1977

Being in the Men's Auxiliary is a necessary but not a sufficient condition for making SCUM's escape list; it's not enough to do good; to save their worthless asses men must also avoid evil. A few examples of the most obnoxious or harmful types are: *rapists*, politicians and all who are in their service (campaigners, members of political parties, etc.); lousy singers and musicians; Chairmen of Boards; Breadwinners; landlords; owners of greasy spoons and restaurants that play Musak; "Great Artists"; cheap pikers; cops; tycoons; scientists working on death and destruction or for private industry (practically all scientists); liars and phonies; disc jockeys; men who intrude themselves in the slightest way on any strange female; real estate men; stock brokers; men who speak when they have nothing to say; men who loiter idly on the street and mar the landscape with their presence; double dealers; flim-flam artists; litterbugs; plagiarizers; men who in the slightest way harm any female [etc.].

Valerie Solanas, *SCUM Manifesto*, 1967

Battle Ground, Wash.: A man dressed as a delivery person entered the home of a 76-year-old woman Friday afternoon and attempted to force the woman to perform sexual acts, but was apparently rebuffed by the woman's stubbornness, the Clark County sheriff's office reported.

The woman was listed in satisfactory condition at Vancouver Memorial Hospital, being treated for bruises, minor stab wounds, and scrapes. . . .

[When] the man demanded she engage in sexual activities, the woman told her attacker, "I'm too old for that sort of thing," police said.

"She said she then turned down the hall and was going to the bathroom where she could lock herself in," a deputy reported.

Then the man picked up from a hallway table an inch-long knife the victim used for opening letters and threatened the victim with that, again demanding she engage in sexual acts, deputies said.

The woman told police she told the man, "That knife is too dull to cut anything."

The assailant knocked the woman to the floor and again attempted to coerce her into sexual acts. She bit him. The woman said the man took out a flashlight and hit her several times.

The man then left.

    The Oregonian, June 24, 1978

I've been working up in McKenzie. I've spent three months there, and boy, I'm sure hard up for a woman. Do you have time?

Shannon stared at him, while driving at 50 mph over the Granville Street bridge. It always made them uncomfortable.

Well, he said, I have an hour before the plane leaves and I sure am hard up for a woman.

There's hookers all over Davie and Granville, Shannon said at last. I'm a cab-driver.

Oh, I wasn't meaning you were a hooker. I wouldn't pay for it. Shit. . . .

A pig like you had better be prepared to pay, Shannon said, because you sure the hell will never get it for free.

Perverts are very sensitive. What did I do to you? he asked, hurt. Why are you insulting me?

You don't consider you insulted me?

No. Shit, no. I mean—You're a dame—And I'm not one of your ordinary construction workers, you know, I'm a *student*.

Helen Potrebenko, *Taxi*, 1975

Headline: *Armed Women Decoys in Campus Rapist Hunt* (Evanston, Ill.).

San Francisco *Chronicle*, June 9, 1973

Ann Arbor Women's Crisis Center puts out booklet, "Freedom from Rape," 1973

Los Angeles, February 1972 Anti-Rape Squad

Seattle, Anti-Rape Squad, 1972

Washington, D.C., Rape Crisis Center, 1973

North Virginia, Task Force on Rape, 1973

June 2, 1974. Two bills before Congress to establish a National Center for the Prevention and Control of Rape

Boston area members of Women Against Rape have established a 24-hour rape crisis center

The *Spokeswoman*, June 15, 1973

"Women, Rape and the Law"
A Community Service Program
Saturday, June 2, 1973
Palm Beach Junior College Gymnasium
Lake Worth, Fla.

The rape laws and the literature concerning them have been dominated by fears that false rape charges might result in the convictions of innocent men. The false complaint is feared more in rape cases than in other crimes because of the basic assumption that many women are either amoral or hostile to men and that women can induce rape convictions solely by virtue of fabricated reports. The commentators, however, consistently have failed to document or closely analyze these assumptions. Nevertheless, these fears have produced and sustained laws and attitudes that seek to protect the innocent from an unjust rape conviction, rather than to protect women from rape.

Camille E. LeGrand, *California Law Review*, 1973, 61

Madison, Wis.: When a 15-year-old boy raped a girl in a stairwell at West High School, Judge Archie Simonson ruled, he was reacting "normally" to prevalent sexual permissiveness and womens' provocative clothing.

The judge decreed that the youth—who was ruled a delinquent—should be permitted to stay at home under court supervision rather than placed in an institution or other rehabilitation center.

Yesterday about 40 women, one wearing a bikini, paraded outside Dane County Courthouse demanding the judge's resignation.

San Francisco *Chronicle*, May 27, 1977

[Judge Simonson] claimed nationwide support yesterday for his views on rape and told women to stop wearing provocative outfits and teasing men. . . .

"I'm trying to say to women, 'stop teasing,' " the judge added.

"There should be a restoration of modesty in dress and the elimination from the community of the sexual gratification businesses."

The 16-year-old victim was wearing tennis shoes, blue jeans and a blouse over a turtleneck sweater when she was attacked by three boys. Her screams for help were drowned out by the school band, rehearsing in a room near the stairwell.

San Francisco *Chronicle*, May 28, 1977

[Judge Simonson] said yesterday his views on sex may be old-fashioned but he vowed not to resign despite the recall move against him.
San Francisco *Chronicle,* July 30, 1977

The concept of victim precipitation hinges primarily on male definitions of expressed or implied consent to engage in sexual relations, and is shaped by traditional restrictive stereotypes of women. Thus, hitchhiking and walking alone at night in a rough neighborhood may be considered behavior encouraging a sexual attack. This view of what a *man* can assume to be a sexual invitation is unreasonable, but is so well engrained in society that women often accept it as well. As a result, a woman may react to being raped with considerable guilt and refuse to report the attack. A woman hitchhiker may later feel that she encouraged the rape simply by accepting a ride. Yet, when the female hitchhiker first sets out to get a ride, she normally is not expecting—or hoping for—a sexual encounter. A woman should not be made to feel guilty for acts that do not involve express sexual invitation, nor should she be denied the right to change her mind. In its failure to accord any consideration to the woman victim's intentions, victim precipitation becomes nothing more than a male view of the circumstances leading up to the incident.
Camille E. LeGrand, *California Law Review,* 1973, 61

[Judge Simonson]: Even in open court we have people appearing—women appearing without bras and with the nipples fully exposed, and they think it is smart and they sit here on the witness stand with their dresses up over the cheeks of their butts, and we have this type of thing in the schools. . . .
Meryl Manhardt [prosecutor]: Your Honor, with all due respect, I find your remarks about women's clothing particularly sexist.
S.: You bet it is. I can't go around walking exposing my genitals like they can the mammary glands.
M.: You are reflecting the general theory that woman provokes an assault, and I cannot accept that idea.

S.: It sure raises a lot of interest in my mind from time to time.
San Francisco *Chronicle*, August 26, 1977

Dane County voters decide today whether to remove Judge Archie Simonson from the bench for controversial remarks he made during a hearing on a juvenile rape case.

Simonson, 52, faces five opponents in a special election that could make him the first state official ousted from office since the recall amendment was adopted in 1926.
San Francisco *Chronicle*, September 7, 1977

"I wanted to be a lawyer because I believed if they chose to, they could make some differences," said Moria Krueger, the Dane County judge-elect, who had just won Wisconsin's first judicial recall election and will become the first woman elected judge in this capital city. . . .

She will take the seat of Archie Simonson [who was recalled Wednesday]. She also trounced four other candidates.

Simonson, 52, lost to Krueger by 8,809 votes out of 77,907 cast in the election.
San Francisco *Chronicle*, September 9, 1977

The fear of the maniac and the genuine desire to protect chaste, totally innocent women from sexual assault clash mightily with the fear of convicting innocent men. As a result, we have on one hand harsh penalties for rape; on the other, however, we have few convictions and a myriad of laws and attitudes that tend to protect men from conviction.
Camille E. LeGrand, *California Law Review,* 1973, 61

Rape is a crime that is still very much with us; in fact, its growth rate is the highest of any violent crime—murder, robbery, and aggravated assault included.

The most recent FBI statistics reveal that reported rapes doubled from 27,620 in 1967 to an all-time high of 56,730 in 1976.
Sandy Hotchkiss, San Francisco *Chronicle*, December 3, 1978

One out of three women over the age of 14 will be raped sometime during her lifetime in Los Angeles County—according to statistics of the Los Angeles Ad Hoc Committee on Rape.

The RAPE CRISIS HOTLINE covers Los Angeles and the San Fernando Valley with 24-hour crisis counselling, information, support and referral. Counselors also accompany victims to the police, hospital and court upon request.
Sister, December 77/January 78

At first we were nameless, a group of friends responding to need: a woman who'd been threatened and assaulted by a former lover, was staying with a friend, but wanted to stay in her own home and was afraid to stay alone. We—7 or 8 of us—set up a schedule, 2 women a night for company and protection.

The results were cheerful but chaotic. This small group decided to set up a structure, a phone list, and a system to offer protection to women being threatened by abusive men. The plan was to stay with the women (mostly at night) in rotating groups of however many women the situation seemed to demand. . . .

Originally we were a confidential, closed group, partly because we were unsure of the legality of what we were doing; partly because we didn't want the abusive men we were protecting the women against to know who we were. This second level of confidentiality—our individual identities—still makes sense to us. About legal implications, we've discovered that when we go into a woman's home at her invitation, we are perfectly within the law.
The Godmothers: A Brief History (pamphlet), Portland, Oregon, March 16, 1978 (written by Melanie Kaye/Kantrowitz)

Rape Speak-Out, July 1972, San Francisco, downtown YWCA

Minneapolis Rape Counseling Center, 1973

Rape Crisis Center, Boston, publishes booklet: "Rape: Medical and Legal Information," 1973

Dade County, Florida, January 10, 1974, Jackson Memorial Hospital Rape Treatment Center opened

We've been talking around the office about some of the terms we use to describe the crimes which our work is against. *Wife abuse*, for example, is inaccurate and leaves out women abused by their sons, brothers, fathers, and boyfriends. *Battered woman* seems to some of us objectifying; think of calling a woman who's been raped a *raped woman*, as if the crime committed against her had somehow transformed her essence. Some of us feel the same way about using the term *victim* excessively, that the word assumes a split between us-on-call and them-calling. In fact many women working on the hotline have been victimized, and none of us would be here if we didn't feel strongly about our potential victimization. *Women victimized by family violence* seems the least offensive term, but it is cumbersome.

Incest is another problem term. Adult cousins or siblings choosing to relate sexually are clearly not the same as a grown man sexually abusing a girl child whose home he has access to, who may or may not be his kin. There should be a word that means "sexual abuse of a girl child by a male relative or pararelative."

There should also be one word that means "violence—sexual or not—against women." In a woman's language, there would be such a word (as the Eskimos have 14 or 18 words for snow).

    Rape Relief Hotline Newsletter (Portland, Oregon), November 1977 (written by Melanie Kaye/Kantrowitz)

It did flash through my mind, while I was in the cage. I remembered how I felt right after I was raped. I changed the way I dressed, where I went; I did everything I could not to be at all alluring or vulnerable in terms of my body as a woman, if I was in a public place where men would be present. So doing that performance in that cage was a cathartic thing for me. There I was doing, full out—being out there, full out, in front of men. And the safety in it was the fact that the cage was there. . . .

It was so marvelous to me, inside, it was like I was doing everything that I wasn't supposed to do, and I was doing it to the most extreme. It was like breaking all the rules of being a woman that the society sets up.

> Interview with Arina Isaacson, performing artist, on her performance with other women in a monkey cage at the San Francisco Zoo, July 1978

> we stand in a circle
> we face out into the dark
> we face danger
> we're not afraid
> we are so many
> we reclaim the night
>
>   . . .
>
> we make this vow
> to ourselves and each other
> to our daughters
> we will extend this safe circle
> until its boundaries dissolve
> and its power is everywhere
> and we are safe everywhere
> all women safe everywhere

> RITUAL: Portland Women's Night Watch 2nd Annual Flashlight March to Stop Violence Against Women and Children, August 25, 1978, in Melanie Kaye/Kantrowitz, *We Speak in Code*, 1979

I often notice that the mirror reflects an image which makes me question myself, feel critical or dissatisfied with my appearance. I don't ignore it as trivial, because I recognize that the mirror is infested with a very common political poison, virus hollywoodius or televisioniensis, subtle pressure to measure up to a pattern designed to enslave. Just to free myself of that pressure isn't a magical operation. But hundreds of other women will use that mirror. So after I have cleared my own image of that false cloud, I usually perform some sort of magical activity to neutralize the poison. I pour suggestive energy into the mirror, encouraging anyone who might look in it to see herself in her true beauty. I reinforce the suggestion with all the power of my will and call on the Goddess of Beauty Herself, blessed Aphrodite, to banish that which would deny Her, as she exists in all of us.

Margi Gumpert, *Country Women*, April 1974

At least 20 films during the last two years served rape to their audiences. In almost none of those films has the rape been more than a plot point, a quick way of getting from here to there—of motivating a distraught husband or lover to kill rapists. Often, it has been less.

Aljean Hurmetz, San Francisco *Chronicle*, October 28, 1973

It is probably true that castration would stop the rapist being a rapist, and would stop the bugger from menacing small boys. It is wholly unlikely that the operation would turn such people into well-adjusted members of society.

New Statesman, October 27, 1967

Two very successful revues have been staged by a group of women who have formed the Westbeth Playwrights Collective in Manhattan. Rape-In, their first show, began as a workshop project last year and was suggested by a man in the then mixed group. But it was the women who completed the assignment. When they did, they discovered they were all feminists.

Rape-In was divided into halves—women as victims and women as aggressors. A scene by Dolores Walker portrayed the offstage rape of a construction worker by a band of harpies. "Our consciousness was raised by the show," Dolores reports. "We saw that in the second half, some of the women acted not only aggressively but negatively. What we were doing was copying the male power structure. So we decided that in the next show—Up!—we would evolve it further."

Ms., August 1972

I look down at the city
which meant life to me, not death
and think that somewhere there
a cold center, composed
of pieces of human beings
metabolized, restructured
by a process they do not feel
is spreading in our midst
and taking over our minds
a thing that feels neither
guilt nor rage: that is unable
to hate, therefore to love.
　　Adrienne Rich, from "Merced," *Diving into the Wreck*, 1973

　Humanity has never shown any regret for this horror [witch-burning] in its cultural works . . . and no calling for an accounting has occurred for us as it did for the Jews at Nuremburg. All women are still seen as witches, and the fear of us has made it nearly impossible to ascend into a love of our own sex.
　　Z. Budapest, *Plexus*, November 1978

Death and disfiguration.

One Christmas eve my lovers and I
we left the bar, driving home slow
there was a woman lying in the snow
by the side of the road. She was wearing
a bathrobe and no shoes, where were
her shoes? she had turned the snow
pink, under her feet. She was an Asian
woman, didn't speak much English, but
she said a taxi driver beat her up
and raped her, throwing her out of his
car
what on earth was she doing there
on a street she helped to pay for
but doesn't own?
doesn't she know to stay home?

I am a pervert, therefore I've learned
to keep my hands to myself in public
but I was so drunk that night,
I actually did something loving
I took her in my arms, this woman,
until she could breathe right, and
my friends who are perverts too
they touched her too
we all touched her.
"You're going to be all right"
we lied. She started to cry
"I'm 55 years old" she said
and that said everything.

Six big policemen answered the call
no child *in* them.
they seemed afraid to touch her.
then grabbed her like a corpse and heaved her
on their metal stretcher into the van,
crashing and clumsy.
She was more frightened than before.
they were cold and bored.
'don't leave me' she said.
'she'll be all right' they said.
  Judy Grahn, from A *Woman is Talking to Death*, 1974

But how hard it is, when we are struggling with fears, to think beyond ourselves and the present moment. Even the most responsible of us is not in a learning mood on those days, days which sometimes stretch into years, years when the quiet voice of reason is drowned out by the cries of the terrorized child within us. Time is meaningless then. How can we master it enough to swing our intelligence up and down the decades, the centuries, scanning them to see what marks our acts are leaving on them?
  Lillian Smith, *The Journey*, 1965

This is a tape about rape we're making. It began because Nellie and I were once talking as we were waiting for the elevator. We were saying how we were so scared just to live alone, and we just had tremendous fear of anything happening at night and in the apartment. We discovered that the reason we were both scared was because we had both been raped and that being raped had long-lasting effects on us.

Noreen Connell and Cassandra Wilson (Eds.), *Rape: The First Sourcebook for Women*, 1974

A five-year follow-up study of rape victims, completed by Dr. Ann Burgess of Boston College and Lynda L. Homstrom, indicates that rape recovery periods vary according to the type of attack a woman experiences. Recovery periods researched in the study lasted from a few months to over five years. Data shows that victims of a random attack take much longer to recover than those who can make some rational explanation for what happened to them.

Those who have the worst time recovering are women who are attacked in their own beds and women deprived of social and emotional support.

One unexpected finding in the study reveals that victims who coped successfully in the past with the loss of a parent or child recovered faster than those without such a history.

The overwhelming majority of the women were profoundly affected by their rape. Forty-two percent rated it as the most upsetting event of their lives.

The Longest Revolution, June 1978

Mind is the soul, mind against fear is a faith dealer and does not smell the alarming animal.

Georgette Cerutti, "That Bone Place Where There Is Light," *Conditions*, II, 1977

Having witch craft, the craft of witches, is having power over your own life. That is why it is and always has been dangerous to the state, the system.

Alice Molloy, *In Other Words*, 1977

We take as our source the hitherto unrecognized culture of women, a culture which from long experience of oppression developed an intense appreciation for life, a sensitivity to unspoken thoughts and the complexity of simple things, a powerful knowledge of human needs and feelings.

    Redstockings of the Women's Liberation Movement, "Principles," 1971

To re-source is to find another source, an entirely different and prior one, a source deeper than the partriarchy and one that allows us to stand in the path of continuous and cosmic energy.

    Sally Gearhart "Through the Looking Glass," keynote address, Women's Spirituality Conference, April 1976, Boston, in *Womanspirit*, Summer 1976

This new spiritual inquiry has challenged and further broken down patriarchal authority—the authority of patriarchal science and religion. At the same time, this broadening of our vision of reality cannot help but have a formative and creative impact on the development of our female culture—as inspiration and material for our art, music, literature, esthetics, *and* by adding a profound new dimension to our relations with one another.

    Susan Rennie and Kirsten Grimstad, *Quest*, Spring 1975

That women in the United States and elsewhere have begun to claim sacred space for themselves, to create rituals which emphasize their loyalty to each other and finally name the powers which men have found "anomalous" (i.e., nameless) is indeed an ultimate, radical (proceeding from the root) affirmation of the revolutionary potential of the feminist movement. Asserting the right to ritual means as a source of power, vision and solidarity is the symbolic corollary of equal pay, choice of abortion, domestic freedom, the establishment of women's businesses, etc. Successful and enduring change in the status of women will come only through the parallel transformation of symbols and realities. Feminist ritual practice is currently the most important model for symbolic and, therefore, psychic and spiritual change in women.

Kay Turner, *Heresies*, Spring 1978

Two trucks driving on the road. Is this real? Ignore it, it will go away. Headlights piercing the soft moonlight, engines roaring, drunken men's shouts. Women's heads turn. . . . Fear ripples through the crowd. . . . "A cone of white light." Women surrounded the circle, the campsites, with white light. Women chanted low and quiet, gradually building in energy. Women stayed in the circle. The drummers kept drumming. "Don't give them any energy." Women softly chanting. "Go away. Go away." Women visualizing the truck keeping going, not stopping, going out. A giant hand pushing the truck down the road. . . . And the truck drove on past us and out, never stopping. The other truck finally got started and roared away. One of the men fell out, ran after the truck shouting, "Don't leave me! Don't leave me!"

Hallie Iglehart, *Womanspirit*, Fall 1975

Most women interested or involved in feminist concepts of spirituality do not regard this spirituality as an end in itself but as a means of gaining and giving strength and understanding that will help us to confront the many tangible and material issues of the blatant inequalities of society as we know it today.

Merlin Stone, *Heresies*, Spring 1978

My name is Wanda Carr. I am 40 years old. My husband beat and abused me for years. I shot him. I was acquitted. California.

ALL: I AM A WOMAN. I FOUGHT BACK.

My name is Marlene Roan Eagle. I am an Oglala Sioux and I am 20 years old. My husband beat me several times. Twice I was hospitalized from these beatings, once for a month. When I was 7 months pregnant, he beat me with a broom handle. I grabbed a knife and stabbed him. I was found not guilty, on grounds of defense of my unborn child. Ohio.

ALL: I AM A WOMAN. I FOUGHT BACK.

My name is Inez Garcia. I killed the man who held me down while his friends raped me. I spent 19 months in prison, my case was 3 years in the courts. I was found not guilty. California.

ALL: I AM A WOMAN. I FOUGHT BACK.

My name is Gloria Maldonado. I am 32 years old. When my husband attacked me and our son, I shot him. I was not prosecuted, on grounds of "insufficient evidence." Chicago, Illinois.

ALL: I AM A WOMAN. I FOUGHT BACK.

My name is Virginia Tierce. I shot the man who raped me. I was found guilty of manslaughter. I was granted a retrial. I was acquitted.

ALL: I AM A WOMAN. I FOUGHT BACK.

> RITUAL: Portland Women's Night Watch 2nd Annual Flashlight March to Stop Violence Against Women and Children, August 25, 1978 in Melanie Kaye/Kantrowitz, *We Speak in Code,* 1979. Parts were read by eight women in masks.

And I've learned once again that the stronger we become, the more demands are made on us. The more healing we learn, the more seriously in need are the people who come to us. The more visibly powerful and loving we become, the more threatening we are to a society that functions by keeping people, and especially women, powerless and alienated from one another.

Hallie Iglehart, *Womanspirit,* Fall 1975

Some feminists see themselves as exclusively "political feminists" or as "spiritual feminists," and many find it difficult to understand the other's point of view. The spiritualists feel that the politicalists are too narrow or insensitive to what they regard as "a more encompassing feminist consciousness," whereas the politicalists consider the spiritualists impractical and believe that they avoid "the reality of the real political issues." I think that it is extremely important for us to realize that this division between the spiritual and the political is arbitrary and unnecessarily divisive.

Judith Todd, *Heresies,* Spring 1978

In putting together this issue on the Great Goddess, Women's Spirituality, we wanted to offer a holistic concept of the Goddess and to move beyond an inside/outside duality. We also recognized a need to counter the distrust that most women harbor towards religion and any aspect of spirituality because of the oppression that we have all experienced from patriarchal religions.
        Editorial Statement, *Heresies*, Spring 1978

It is the object and center of the whole Law to abolish idolatry and utterly uproot it, and to overthrow the opinion that any of the stars could interfere for good or evil in human matters, because it leads to the worship of stars. It was therefore necessary to slay all witches as being undoubtedly idolators. . . . But in all performances of witchcraft it is laid down as a rule that women should be employed in the chief operation; and therefore the Law says, "Thou shalt not suffer a witch to live."
        Maimonides, *The Guide for the Perplexed*, 1956

The first phase of the current battle/war passes: the breaking of the symbolic power of the phallos in crucial areas . . . the overall consciousness of the civilization, at least in this country, is definitely for the first time in our lifetime, questioning that power, if only by virtue of being aware that that is where the center of power is, in this civilization. . . . We have broken that power symbolically in crucial areas.
        Alice Molloy, *In Other Words*, 1977

As Western religions entered a state of alienation from the body, nature and this world, women were denigrated because they seemed more carnal, fleshy, and earthy than the culture creating males. . . . The denigration of the female body and its powers is further expressed in Western culture's attitudes toward childbirth. . . . The women's liberation movement aided the advocates of natural childbirth and home birth by emphasizing the need for women to control and take pride in their bodies.

The symbol of the Goddess aids this process of naming and re-claiming the female body and its functions. In the ancient world and among modern women, the Goddess symbol represents the birth, death, and rebirth processes of the natural and human worlds. The female body is viewed as a direct expression or incar-nation, of waxing and waning, life and death cycles in the universe.
Carol P. Christ, *Heresies*, Spring 1978

Historian Vincent Scully maintains that not even the palaces were of greatest architectural importance on Crete. He believes that their siting in the landscape was more important. Typically each temple, here as well as throughout Greece, was built in an enclosed valley and aligned on a north/south axis to have a view across the valley of a conical hill, and beyond that, to a horned or double-peaked mountain that contained a cave sanctuary. At the Palace of Knossos, these features were sited/sighted through the Horns of Consecration. The proper siting of the palace accentuated the meaning of the landscape as the body of the Goddess. The valley was her encircling arms; the conical hill, her breast or nurturing function; the horned mountains, her "lap" or cleft vulva, the Earth's active power; and the cave sanctuary, her birth-giving womb.
Mimi Lobell, *Heresies*, Spring 1978

For as regards intellect, or the understanding of spiritual things, they seem to be of a different nature from men.
Heinrich Kramer and James Sprenger, *Malleus Maleficarum*, 1971 (orig. pub. 1486)

Long before the influential oracular site of Delphi was seized by Apollo, it was a sacred part of the body of the Earth Mother Gaea. From a seismic cleft in this "body of Gaea," exuded intoxicating gases that induced prophetic visions. Apollo killed the great Python, protector of the site; thereafter Pythia, the priestess who pronounced the prophecies, spoke for Apollo rather than Gaea.
Mimi Lobell, *Heresies*, Spring 1978

We found wherever there are feminist communities, women are exploring psychic and nonmaterial phenomena; reinterpreting astrology; creating and celebrating feminist rituals around birth, death, menstruation; reading the Tarot; studying prepatriarchal forms of religion; reviving and exploring esoteric goddess-centered philosophies such as Wicce; developing and cultivating dream analysis, ESP, astral projection, precognition; learning psychic and homeopathic healing; rescuing the holistic perspective of the right hemisphere of the brain from the contempt of the left-brained linear-mindedness; practicing meditation and yoga; rewriting the *I Ching*; revolutionizing our food and natural resource consciousness of our connectedness with the rest of the biosphere.

    Susan Rennie and Kirsten Grimstad, *Quest*, Spring 1975

Thus the witches sometimes order: take a leaf of a certain plant, when the moon is seen in a certain degree . . . also a certain quantity of the horn, the sweat, the hair, and blood of a certain animal when the sun is, e.g., in the middle of the sky . . . and a portion of a certain mineral . . . melted at a certain conjunction of sun and moon, and a definite position of the stars; speak then, and say certain words, and fumigate with those leaves . . . to that molten image, and such and such a thing will happen. . . . In most cases the condition is added that women must perform these actions. Thus it is stated in reference to the means of obtaining rain that ten virgins dressed with diadems and red garments should dance.

    Maimonides, *The Guide for the Perplexed*, 1956

It has emerged from feminist consciouness, an inkling or more of the first aspect and perhaps ever-present search for answers to such theological questions as the possible purposes (or nonpurpose) of existence, the true nature of morality (or immorality), birth, death, and the nature of the mind as it is revealed in intelligence, intuition, and reason. For many centuries, women have been taught that if they cared to consider these questions at all (the implication being that such questions were actually too abstract for

female minds) answers were to be found in the words and writings of male priests, male ministers, male rabbis and male gurus.
Merlin Stone, *Heresies*, Spring 1978

On the most immediate level, in my work, I am trying to write poems that are free of the institutionalized conflicts and brutality that have characterized our literary tradition for so long, to use simple grammar and syntax, and to praise, praise.
Olga Broumas, *Heresies*, Fall 1977

I told of my experiences with the grove of trees from which Ruth and I have taken our names. The place was a meditation/intuition source for us for three years until we were forced to leave the commune because of our feminist politics. We had developed simple silent rituals and agreed not to change anything in the grove. Without realizing it, in these ways we were creating a space for intuition to come to us. I began to embrace trees and listen for guidance, but then condemned myself for this freaky behavior. Ruth supported my continuing it and encouraged me to write down what I "heard" there. These records in my journals have been very helpful.
Jean Mountaingrove, *Womanspirit*, Summer 1976

In authentic ritual experience, something, an ability to break through the present, is available which can lead to discovery and creativity. Ritual is a potent source of invention because the participants feel the extreme intensity, sometimes the ecstasy, of openness to possibility and revelation. This sense of extreme openness and creativity is rare for women who have been traditionally circumscribed by severe limitation, constrained by custom, with no hope for a changed future.
Kay Turner, *Heresies*, Spring 1978

Some say they find this force within themselves; others regard it as external. Some feel it in the ocean, the moon, a tree, the flight of a bird or in the constant stream of coincidences (or noncoincidences) that occur in our lives. Some find access to it in the lighting of a candle, chanting, meditating alone or with other women . . .

Merlin Stone, *Heresies*, Spring 1978

Spirituality is so threatening because it is absolutely predicated upon self-trust.

Juanita Weaver, *Womanspirit*, Fall 1975

She looked up over her knitting and met the third stroke and it seemed to her like her own eyes meeting her own eyes, searching as she alone could search into her mind and her heart, purifying out of existence that lie, any lie. She praised herself in praising the light, without vanity, for she was stern, she was searching, she was beautiful like that light. It was odd, she thought, how if one was alone, one leant to inanimate things; trees, streams, flowers; felt they expressed one; felt they became one; felt they knew one, in a sense were one; felt an irrational tenderness thus (she looked at that long steady light) as for oneself.

Virginia Woolf, *To the Lighthouse*, 1927

Connections are made slowly, sometimes they grow underground.
You cannot tell always by looking what is happening.
More than half a tree is spread out in the soil under your feet.

Marge Piercy, from "The Influence Coming into Play: The Seven of Pentacles," *To Be of Use*, 1973

Now, think over what I'm saying. There may be a way to help us get back. The medicine is dangerous, in which lies its power. Stand before a mirror. Just keep eye contact until you've said hello. Rest on the stream of feeling flowing through your eyes. Know the safety of that place where you ARE all change. Cry in your face—hurting sorrow. Cross your hands and begin to touch—life starts to flow. Masturbate to water roses, feel the color come. Cross your eyes a new dimension. Vision of the Eye. Twinkling lights dance over the surface. Through the mirror to the other side. The Goddess is you, in your image.

The gift of the Goddess is body to soul, soul to body. Imagine the energy if we all looked at once. The Patriarchy could not stand such a blow. They took our bodies away by forbidding the looking. They said we were objects and they had the eyes. But they can never kill Her, only try to get us to knock ourselves off. And we'll never do it. Her reflections are scattered through their dark halls.

Remember the past. The Goddess grows restless. All alone I can't stand the heat of Her energy. Help me, sisters. Look in the mirror.
    Martha Alsup, *Heresies*, Spring 1978

As women we are coming to know the power of consciousness— it is energy that participates in the coalescence of the events that happen to us. From the beginning of each of our lives, we've been systematically trained to experience ourselves as vulnerable, as weak sexual objects. No longer can we allow ourselves to feel like victims only to attract those looking for a likely object. We must dig deep into the roots of our experience, extract all these feelings and throw them into the face of the patriarchy; replacing them with our strength and power, thereby entering a new dimension of life— leaving all rapists behind with no victims to be found.
    Margo Adair, teacher of applied meditation

Every three minutes a woman is beaten by her male partner— a man who often claims to love her. Every five minutes a woman is raped, and they call that "making love" too. And every ten minutes a little girl is molested, sometimes by a relative, perhaps her own father. The violence mounts. . . .
    Donna Warnock, "Patriarchy Is a Killer: What People Concerned About Peace and Justice Should Know," 1981 from *Reweaving the Web of Life*, ed. Pam McAllister, 1982

I told adults of the horror I was enduring, but NO ONE listened. Or they believed that my parents were such pillars of the community that they could not be guilty of the crime. Later, therapists referred to Oedipal fantasies instead of listening to what I was saying.

Jill Morgan, "It Began For Me," *I Never Told Anyone: Writings by Women Survivors of Child Sexual Abuse*, 1983

That these tragedies are so overlooked and unappreciated as the horrible acts of war they are is testimony to how much damage has already been done in the hearts and minds of the people.

Donna Warnock, "Patriarchy Is a Killer," 1981

I never told anyone: Why is it that children who have been molested, sexually abused, or even raped rarely ever tell? They never tell for the same reason that anyone who has been helplessly shamed and humiliated, and who is without protection or validation of personal integrity, prefers silence.

Florence Rush, "Foreward," *I Never Told Anyone*, 1983

The horror of nuclear weapons and the possibility of nuclear war had frightened and worried me . . . for years. . . . I had a feeling that many women felt as I did . . . and finally put an advertisement in *Spare Rib*, asking women to contact me if they had dreams about nuclear war. All through that summer in 1980, I received letter after letter from women talking about their own bad dreams.

Alice Cook, "A Private Nightmare," *Greenham Women Everywhere*, 1983

And life, which means everything to me, becomes meaningless, because these celebrations of cruelty destroy my very capacity to feel and to care and to hope. I hate the pornographers most of all for depriving me of hope.

Andrea Dworkin, "Pornography and Grief," speech presented at the Feminist Perspectives on Pornography Conference, before a Take Back the Night March, 1978

I was in a jeep driving through a very wasted landscape but I knew it was a long time after a nuclear war. . . . The atmosphere was very thick. I couldn't see any stars, but the headlights of the jeep were working. . . . My friend was driving, and I was holding between my knees a giant piece of ice. Inside the block there was a fish, and this was the last fish, which I had to get to London . . . where there was still some clear water. . . .

This fish I was holding was the fish of knowledge, and if we could keep the fish alive there was some hope for continuance in the world. But if we couldn't it would be the end.

A dream told by Noa in "A Private Nightmare," *Greenham Women Everywhere*, 1983

It began for me the summer I was four years old. . . . With no words and no warning he spread my legs and entered me dry. My scream started the dog barking. I must have passed out, because my next memory is of the sunlit garden through the French doors . . . and the sound of the dog barking frantically. . . .

When he was through with me, he dropped me on the floor like a discarded dishrag. Then with belt in hand he began beating me. When the belt stopped its endless rise and fall, he took me in the bedroom, redressed me in the same play clothes, and put me in my bed with a strict injunction to stay there.

Jill Morgan, *I Never Told Anyone*, 1983

Gandhi's word for nonviolent action, *satyagraha*, translates as "clinging to the truth." The patriarchy is so clearly founded on lies and more lies that that definition of struggle makes even more sense to me now than before. Though the words *clinging to the truth* are not quite adequate, are they? They would seem to imply that we know the whole truth.

Barbara Deming in a conversation with Mab Segrest, *Reweaving the Web of Life*, 1982

Even if we dismantle the bombs, cement power plants,
ban 2, 4, 5-T, men are still raping women.

Men raped women before they split the atom
before they concocted herbicides in their stainless steel laboratories.

They raped in war and they raped in what they called peace.. . . .
Ellen Bass, *Our Stunning Harvest*, 1986

And women are very aware now that we have to *learn* to use our
own eyes, to refuse just to see what we're told to see.
Barbara Deming, *Reweaving the Web of Life*, 1982

It absolutely boggles my mind what might happen if women
would realize that the dirt in the rivers and oceans as well as the
dirt on the kitchen floor is *our* dirt. What might the planet be like
if all that intelligence, caring endurance, and willingness to sacrifice could be extended from the private domain to planetary consciousness! The hand that rocks the cradle could swing the balance
to the side of survival. . . .
Elissa Melamed, *Mirror, Mirror: The Terror of Not Being Young*, 1983

We came to this action as women and feminists, connecting
crimes against us in our daily lives with the worldwide violence of
the military machine. . . . We acted because we fear for our own
lives and because we oppose the military mentality: that of rule by
the biggest weapons, of penetration and domination, and of appro-
priation of our lives to keep this power structure intact. We see this
military mentality as intimately tied to the oppression and fears we
women live with every day—the fear of rape, the oppression of
having our reproductive choices taken from us, the coercion of
compulsory heterosexuality. . . .
"Why We're Here," statement from Arlington jail by 43 women arrested while 3500 blocked entrances to the Pentagon. In Lynne Jones
(Ed.), *Keeping the Peace*, 1981

Yes. It's true. All true. I am scrupulously accurate. I keep track
of all distinctions. Between past and present. Pain and pleasure.
Living and surviving. Resistance and capitulation. Will and circumstances. Between life and death. Yes. I am scrupulously accurate. I have become a keeper of accounts.
Irena Kelpfisz, *Keeper of Accounts*, 1982

She is immovable. Her face suffering and wondering. "But look," she says, pointing. Four large plastic dolls—one a skinny Farrah Fawcett (or so the doll looks to her) posed for an anal inspection; one an oriental, with her eyes, strangely, closed, but her mouth, a pouting red suction cup, open; an enormous eskimo woman— with fur around her neck and ankles, and vagina; and a Black woman dressed entirely in a leopard skin, complete with tail. The dolls are all life-size, and the efficiency of their rubber genitals is explained in detail on a card visible through the plate glass.

For her this is the stuff of nightmares because all the dolls are smiling.

Alice Walker, "Coming Apart." In Laura Lederer (Ed.), *Take Back the Night*, 1980

We do not have a history of taboos against the sexual use of children. Until recently, children were a paternal property and could be legitimately exploited, sold, or even killed by their masters.

Florence Rush, "Child Pornography," *Take Back the Night*, 1980

While films like *Snuff* "entertain" male viewers, the military has offered hands-on experience. Veteran Hale reports that on the way to Vietnam troops were told, "There's a lot of loose ass over there, men, and they just love GI dick. And best of all, they are only Gooks, so if you get tired of them, you can cram a grenade up their cunt and 'waste' them."

Donna Warnock, *Patriarchy Is a Killer*, 1981

In my view, any commitment to nonviolence which is real, which is authentic, must begin in the recognition of the forms and degrees of violence perpetrated against women by the gender class men.

Andrea Dworkin, *Our Blood*, 1975

Our no to war coincides with our struggle for liberation. Never before have we seen so clearly the connection between nuclear escalation and the culture of the muscleman; between the violence of war and the violence of rape.

Statement by Sicilian women in response to the decision to site Cruise missiles in Comiso, Sicily, 1981

We read on the poster: "The Bloodiest Thing that Ever Happened in Front of a Camera." We saw displayed on Main Street a woman's body cut into pieces by a pair of bloody scissors. This was how they advertised *Snuff*.

Martha Gever and Marg Hall, "Fighting Pornography." In Laura Lederer (Ed.), *Take Back the Night*, 1980

As we got to Downing Street there was hardly any talking, but our senses were very attuned to each other. I asked the policeman on duty a few absurd questions to play for time while we felt out what we wanted to do. We all lay down. A second after I lay down, I looked up at the police staring down at me. Although we'd decided to be completely silent, I found the word *Hallo* slipping out of me. I was cross with myself, for it had come out of weakness and fear. Then I became very calm.

Deborah Law, *Greenham Women Everywhere*, 1983

It seemed appropriate to destroy that poster. It was the least we could do. The next morning four of us went to the theatre, spray painted the doors and chained them shut, put glue in the locks, broke the display window, and ripped up the poster.

Martha Gever and Marg Hall, "Fighting Pornography." *Take Back the Night*, 1980

. . . I felt very clear. It was as if a film had lifted—an actual space had opened up. Through becoming completely limp, not moving, and seemingly abdicating all responsibility (to the police), I felt that it was I who was in control.

Deborah Law, *Greenham Women Everywhere*, 1983

Societies retaining the idea of Goddess worship seldom demonstrate marital or extramarital rape; female sexuality is nearly always fully developed.

Barbara Walker, *The Woman's Encyclopedia of Myths and Secrets,* 1983

Biologically, most women in the world do still vividly experience their embeddedness in Nature and can harbor few illusions concerning their freedom and separatedness from the cycles of birth and death.

Hazel Henderson, "The Warp and the Weft: The Coming Synthesis of Eco-Philosophy and Eco-Feminism." In Leonie Caldecott and Stephanie Leland (Eds.), *Reclaim the Earth,* 1983

This seemed an essentially female way of being: not to stand out against the environment but to integrate with it. The web of lives is bound together by the women, their millions of small actions performed daily and hourly. . . .

Sandy Boucher, *Heartwomen,* 1982

something in the water
the fruit
I have said this before
a metallic taste
or no taste
I have said it

ask all you want to know
my mother tells me
and my questions
sleep with me
until I can say
you have answered and now
it is I who
Susan Griffin, from "On the Edge"

When I speak of the erotic, then, I speak of it as an assertion of the life force of women; of that creative energy empowered, the knowledge and use of which we are now reclaiming in our language, our history, our dancing, our loving, our work, our lives.

Audre Lorde, *Uses of the Erotic: The Erotic as Power*, 1980

Appendix 1

CURRENT STATISTICS

How many rapes take place each year? Who is raped? Where do these rapes take place? These and other questions are not easy to answer. The same social conditions and attitudes which create rape also make it difficult to assess accurately how often and under what circumstances rape actually takes place. A whole range of misogynist attitudes, including the myth that women want to be raped or that a woman's word is not to be trusted, contribute to the silence of survivors and to prejudice from police, judges and jurors, and others whose task it is to estimate the true proportions of this crime.

The Uniform Crime Report, for example, which is often quoted as an authoritative source, bases its estimate of rape on the numbers of rapes reported to the police. It does not include unreported rapes. Even reported rapes are excluded from this estimate because they have been called "unfounded" by police who have dismissed them as false reports. And if a rape is not officially recorded by the police (because, for instance, a man accused of rape was tried for an offense other than rape) this rape is not included in the Uniform Crime Report's statistics.

Even according to the Uniform Crime Report, the incidence of rape has almost doubled over the last decade. This report comparing current statistics with statistics from 1974 lists an increase of 42.5%.

Even according to the Uniform Crime Report the rate of rape has continually increased more or decreased less than other violent crimes. Before 1981 the rate of increase of rape was higher than for murder or aggravated assault. Since 1981 there has been a decrease in the incidence of all violent crime, but rape either has not decreased at all (from 1982–83, for example) or it has decreased far less than other violent crimes.

The Uniform Crime Report would place the incidence of rape far below the incidence of aggravated assault. (In 1983, according to this report, 78,920 rapes were committed as opposed to 639,530 cases of aggravated assault.) But this data by itself is not satisfactory because of large numbers of rapes that go unreported, are considered unfounded, or are not officially recorded.

Estimates of the number of rapes reported out of the number of rapes actually occurring have ranged from 50 to less than 5%. A recent study conducted in 1978 by Diana H. Russell* estimates that reported rapes represent about 9.5% of all rapes committed. Because of the thoroughness and sensitivity of this study, this figure represents the most reliable evidence available. The figures in the Russell survey were drawn from interviews with an independently selected cross section of women. Those who conducted these interviews were carefully trained and their questions were carefully written to avoid sexual bias and to encourage the trust necessary for women to reveal whether or not they had been raped.

In the light of the Russell survey, to achieve a more accurate idea of the number of rapes committed in 1983, one must multiply the figure of 78,920 by a factor of ten, at least, and this places the number of rapes far above the number of cases of aggravated assault (even if it is taken into account that some cases of aggravated assault also go unreported).

Another study conducted in 1979 indicates that this figure should be increased by still another factor. In 1979 Thomas McCahill, Linda Meyer, and Arthur Fischman found that 56% of reported rapes were not *recorded* as rapes in the Uniform Crime Reports for that city.

Extrapolating from that study, one would have to double the number of rapes reported in the Uniform Crime Report before mul-

---

*I am grateful to Diana H. Russell, *Sexual Exploitation, Rape, Child Sexual Abuse, and Workplace Harassment* (Beverly Hills, 1984) for a clear presentation of her study and for many insights regarding statistics on rape in general.

tiplying that figure by a factor of ten, accounting for unrecorded as well as unreported rapes, to reach the figure of 1,578,400 rapes committed in 1983. This figure is, of course, only an estimate, as are all figures with regard to rape. But it is an estimate that far more accurately reflects the experience of most women who must deal with the threat and danger of violence both practically and emotionally every day.

The Russell survey is also illuminating regarding the increase in the rate of rape. According to this study, the likelihood of a woman being raped during her lifetime has steadily increased. Of women interviewed who were between the ages of 50 and 59, 33.9% had been raped. Of those between 40 and 49, 46.2% had been raped; of those between 30 and 39, 58.7% had been raped; and, most alarmingly, between the ages of 18 and 29, 53.2% had already been raped.

Extrapolating from data provided by the National Crime Survey, the Bureau of Justice Statistics Bulletin for March 1985, gives us the following profile of the crime of rape from 1973 until 1982. Of all reported rapes, 29% occurred in a home or vacation home, 5% took place in a commercial building, 2% in schools, 7% near home, 39% on the street, in a park, playground, parking lot or garage, and 17% in other places. According to the same bulletin, of women who were raped in those years, 43% came from families with an income below $7,499. Another 10% came from families with incomes from $10,000 to $14,999. An additional 31% came from families with incomes from $15,000 to $24,999. And only 8% came from families with an income over $25,000. The same bulletin reports a disproportionately higher rate of rape for black women than for white women compared to the number of black women in the population.

Unlike the Uniform Crime Report, the National Crime Survey bases its figures on interviews. However, one questions the veracity of these interviews when one discovers, for example, that this study failed to uncover even a single case of rape committed in San Jose,

California, in 1970. This failure to discover rape most probably occurred, as Diana Russell has pointed out, because of the kind of questions that were asked. None of the questions posed in this study ever used the word *rape* explicitly, nor did they describe the act of rape as such.

Although a number of studies have come to the conclusion that the rate of rape is higher for poor women than for middle- or upper-class women, the Russell survey, again, challenges these findings. According to the Russell survey women from upper middle-class families are the most likely to be raped.

The Russell survey departs in this and other conclusions about rape from other studies because the interviews conducted in this study revealed the frequency of rapes committed by husbands, intimates, and others who were not strangers to their victims. According to the Russell survey, although more lower-class women were raped by strangers, far more middle- and upper middle-class women were raped by men who were not strangers to them. Earlier studies have omitted this category of rape because of the nature of their questions.

In a similar way, many other studies have come to the conclusion that black women have been raped at a higher rate per capita than white women. But the Russell survey (which also broke down the category of white women into Jewish and non-Jewish) found that rape was nearly equally prevalent in the lives of Jewish, non-Jewish, white, and black women (50, 45 and 44%, respectively). Again Russell found that the difference between her study and other studies is "due to the restriction of prior studies to stranger or acquaintance rape, in contrast to the Russell survey, which uncovered a great deal of rape by intimates as well."

The prevalence of rape, which is part of women's subjective experience and has been reported by many rape crisis clinics as well as the Russell survey, has been confirmed by a recent study of rape on college and university campuses. This study, conducted by Mary

P. Koss,* questioned 7,000 students at a representative sample of 35 schools. It found that 52% of the women surveyed had experienced some form of sexual victimization. One in eight had been raped, according to the legal definition of rape. Koss concluded that "at least ten times more rapes occur among college students than are reflected in official crime statistics."

The Koss study found that a very large percentage, 47%, of the rapes reported to her survey were committed by first or casual dates or by "romantic acquaintances." Just as marital rape and rape by intimates changes the conventional picture of rape in general, the high incidence of rape by men who have dated women changes one's notion, not only of rape, but also of the relationships between young women and men.

This study, like the Russell survey, also calls into question the accuracy of other studies because it reveals how difficult it is for women to speak directly of being raped, or, often, even to perceive a rape as such. Of those women in the study who answered yes to the question of whether they ever had "sexual intercourse against their will through use of threat or force," the legal definition of rape, nearly three quarters did not directly identify their experience as rape.

The denial that surrounds not only violence toward women but also the real social condition of women affects the women who are the victims of rape, as well as police, jurors, and students of crime.

And in the same way, this denial makes it difficult if not impossible to assess accurately how common is the sexual abuse of children. One scholar, David Finkelhorn, has estimated that 75 to 90% of the cases of the sexual abuse of children are not reported. At the same time, just as with rape, there exist many indications that this is a widespread and frequent crime. Judith Lewis Herman

---

*This study by Mary Koss, who is a professor of psychology at Kent State University, Ohio, was sponsored by the Ms. Magazine Campus Project on Sexual Assault. See Ms., October 1985.

studied five American surveys regarding the sexual abuse of children and reported that one third to one fifth of all women questioned had had "some sort of childhood sexual encounter with an adult male." And, as with rape, society's picture of the sexual abuse of children has changed in the last decade to include the understanding of how often children are abused by teachers or friends or family members. Sandra Butler writes in A *Conspiracy of Silence* that in three of four cases reported a child has been abused by someone known and trusted.

What remains evident is that rape, whether it be of adult women or children, is still hidden from our scrutiny. Those who would know the significance and the dimension of this crime must also be students of silence, and ask why and how this silence came to be and is sustained.

Appendix 2

Information about rape and sexual assault can be obtained from the agencies listed below. The 1981 edition of *National Directory: Rape Prevention and Treatment Sources* is published by the National Center for Prevention and Control of Rape and available from the Superintendent of Documents, U.S. Government Printing Office, Washington, DC 20402.

National Center for the Prevention and Control of Rape
National Institute of Mental Health
Room 15–99, Parklawn Building
5600 Fishers Cane
Rockville, MD 20857
(301) 443–3728
(interdisciplinary perspective)

National Center on Child Abuse and Neglect Clearinghouse
P.O. Box 1182
Washington, D.C. 20013
(301) 251–5157
(child sexual assault)

National Criminal Justice Reference Service
P.O. Box 6000
Rockville, MD 20850
(202) 251–5500
(criminal justice perspective)

National Library of Medicine
National Institute of Health

Building 38
8600 Rockville Pike
Bethesda, MD 20894
(301) 496–5116
(bibliographic searches of professional literature)